In the middle of the Atlantic Ocean
is an area known as the Bermuda
triangle which covers approximately
three-hundred thousand square miles
of open sea. Within this comparatively
small patch of ocean more than
a hundred ships and aircraft have been
permanently listed as missing during
the last two centuries – they left no
sign of wreckage, sent no distress
signals . . .

What really happened to these fated
vehicles? Could they have somehow
wandered into an ancient force-field,
left by an alien technology who once
tried to colonize Earth?

Alan and Sally Landsburg found
themselves on the trail of this and other
enigmas of history – colossal temples
and monoliths built by the Incas,
parts from a digital computer dating
from 50 b.c. and the brilliant
architecture of the ancient Egyptians –
when they began their journey –

**IN SEARCH OF ANCIENT
MYSTERIES**

# Alan and Sally Landsburg

# In Search of
# Ancient Mysteries

## Foreword by Rod Serling

**CORGI BOOKS**
A DIVISION OF TRANSWORLD PUBLISHERS LTD

*To Valerie, Michael, their grandmothers,*
*and grandfather and all their ancient ancestors*

# IN SEARCH OF ANCIENT MYSTERIES

A CORGI BOOK 0 552 09588 5

First publication in Great Britain

PRINTING HISTORY
Corgi edition published 1974
Corgi edition reprinted 1975
Corgi edition reprinted 1978

Corgi Books are published by Transworld Publishers Ltd.,
Century House, 61–63 Uxbridge Road,
Ealing, London, W.5.
Made and printed in Great Britain by
Hunt Barnard Printing Ltd., Aylesbury, Bucks.

# Contents

"I always felt that man is a stranger on this planet. A total stranger. I always played with the fancy maybe a contagion from outer space is the seed of man. Hence our prior occupation with heaven, with the sky, with the stars, the gods, somewhere out there, in outer space."

Eric Hoffer

### ACKNOWLEDGMENT

The authors gratefully acknowledge the contributions made by concerned scientists and officials of the following institutions:

Institute for Molecular and Cellular Evolution,
    University of Miami
Foto Servicio Aerofotografico Nacionali, Lima, Peru
National Museum, New Delhi, India
British Museum of Natural History
Peabody Museum, Cambridge
Museo De Oro, Bogota, Colombia
Museo Rafael Larco Herrera, Lima, Peru
Cuzco Archaeological Museum
Museum of Mankind, London


The authors are deeply grateful to Keith Monroe for his invaluable editorial guidance and literary assistance, and to Elizabeth Johnson for her dedicated research efforts.

# Foreword

## by
## Rod Serling

There is a certain uniqueness to my long association with Alan Landsburg. Unlike the usual relationship between writer and producer, we have never threatened each other with bodily harm. And even our artistic disagreements—which are absolutely par for the television course—have been quiet things ended with a mutually satisfying compromise. The reason for this in no way reflects a benign character on my part. I happen to be a screamer, pacer, wall-climber and curtain chewer. Alan Landsburg, on the other hand, is a quiet guy who manages to make his point in a semi-whisper while the echoes of your own shouting still float over the scene.

This is by way of documenting my admiration for an extraordinary young man who has managed to turn many of my literary properties into solid gold by virtue of his taste and his preoccupation with quality.

From "Certain Honorable Men," a two hour-plus television play with Van Heflin, to "A Storm In Summer" with Peter Ustinov, which earned us Emmy recognition for the Best Television Drama of the Year, and on into "The Undersea World of Jacques Cousteau," which Alan produced and I narrated, I found that this thoughtful and energetic producer brought with him judgment and taste of consistent quality. "The March of Time," "The National Geographic

Series," "Biography," "The New Explorers," "On Location," were all productions that stood a cut above the field.

More than a year ago Alan called me and said he wanted to see me about something new that he was getting into, something about visitors from outer space. Frankly, it sounded like something injected through a needle into a major vein. I have always looked to Alan for new and fresh ideas but here I found him vaguely alluding to a "Twilight Zone" type of program, a well plowed field in the demi-world of fantasy, which seemed to me stale and overdone. It was only out of a sense of friendship that I sat down to discuss Alan's "outer space" idea.

My normally articulate friend was babbling incoherently; that was the conclusion I reached after fifteen minutes or so of discussion. As far as I was concerned, we were talking about pure fiction, and spacemen visiting Earth was one of the most outworn themes in the field.

"Rod, I think it's real. I think I can prove that Earth was visited by intelligent life from outer space."

With a sense of sorrow over a reasonably good mind gone sour, I said, "Okay, let's see it."

Item one was a picture of an airfield taken from 2,-500 feet up. "Okay, it's an airfield—from the look of the runways, a military base of some size." That's the impression I got.

"Rod, it's four-thousand years old."

And we were off and running. One after another Alan dug out of his bag pictures taken around the world of places and things that should not have been there. Drawings of electric batteries, spaceships, transistor radios—all dating to pre-history—were the unrelated bits and pieces of evidence that he had assembled. Had it been anyone else showing the objects and pictures to me I might have said "Mountebank!" and tried to find the trick by which the photographs and text were derived. From the years of working with Alan on the Cousteau television series I knew he had more than the amateur's command of the fields of archeology, biology and related scientific investigation. There was no magic involved.

By the time we were finished I had seen enough evidence to convince me that we had entered a new and fascinating field of research. If we kept at it, we would turn up more and more pieces of the puzzle encapsuled in the question: "Where did we come from?"

I now think that it is highly possible that man had his genesis somewhere in outer space. The unsatisfying part of television is that we only have fifty minutes to outline the theory. In the following pages Alan has the time to draw you into his private twilight zone ... and like me, I think you'll be hooked.

# I

## *How Did We Start?*

The camera was ready. A microphone was clipped to Dr. Leslie Orgel's necktie. The crew of technicians was waiting.

For a moment tension tied my tongue. The place was still. There was no visible sign of life in the stark gray walls that towered around us. A thought went through my mind, Silence and lifelessness are appropriate to the theme of this interview. We were going to talk about one of time's best-kept secrets: how did life start on a lifeless Earth?

The secret has always troubled science. The scientist facing me, here in the marble courtyard of the Salk Institute at La Jolla, California, had proposed an answer that might lead to a rethinking of the whole story of mankind.

Dr. Orgel eyed me a bit quizzically, waiting for me to begin. Why must I feel butterflies in my stomach after fifteen years of making documentary films?

Call it the excitement of science and of a strange invention. Great theories in science are always great inventions—products of the imagination. The atom is an invention; the universe is an invention. There are more conceptions of the universe than there are makes of automobiles. Now I was investigating another new theory. I confronted the task of drawing out the theorist carefully and intelligently so that his ideas would come through clearly on a roll of sound film.

A routine beginning would be easiest. I asked him to summarize his career briefly.

"Certainly. Educated at Oxford . . . started as a chemist and moved gradually into biological sciences . . . currently involved in the study of the aging process in individual cells . . ."

He went on—but he didn't mention the brief recent episode in his career that I wanted him to talk about.

He had been coauthor of a paper published in *Icarus*, a monthly devoted to studies of the solar system. It had caused a bemused stir among scientists and attracted my attention. So I asked him about it.

"Francis Crick and I wrote the article more or less for our own amusement."

But some people had taken it seriously. Such authorities as Orgel and Crick (Nobel Prize winner for helping to discover the structure of DNA, the master key to heredity) could hardly be ignored, even when they advanced a theory that sounded bizarre and science fictional. The *Icarus* article had been discussed, explained, and debated in large publications.

To lead Dr. Orgel toward an explanation of his theory, I asked, "Am I correct in thinking that the first living molecule on Earth is generally supposed to have been formed by a chance combination of chemicals, perhaps when they were under bombardment by solar rays or electrical charges of lightning?"

He began, "Of course it's possible that life started spontaneously here on Earth. And if you ask my opinion, I think it's far more likely that it did start here than that it came from somewhere else. But there just isn't the scientific evidence to be sure, and one should maintain an open mind."

"And the alternative possibility, simply put, is that life here originated in outer space?"

"Yes. That possibility shouldn't be regarded as completely silly. The point of our paper wasn't to try to push the origin of life elsewhere, but merely to point out the possibility."

"Wasn't this possibility considered and discarded long ago?"

"In the nineteenth century there were two theories

about how life could have got here from outside. In England Lord Calvin said that life arrived as a spore carried on a meteorite. In Sweden a chemist named Svante Arrhenius suggested that a spore could have been blown directly from a planet in another solar system all the way to Earth. . . ."

One of the keys in my early research had been the work of Arrhenius. He was an eminent scientist who had conceived the concept of ionization. In 1907 he published a book entitled *Worlds in the Making*. It described a universe in which life had always existed and drifted haphazardly through space, occasionally colonizing new planets. This life traveled in the form of spores that escaped from a planet's atmosphere by random movement and then were driven through space by pressure of light from the sun. (Such light pressure had already been demonstrated experimentally.) When the spores fell on a planet, Arrhenius held, they would awaken into active life and compete with life forms already present, or inoculate the planet with life if it was lifeless but habitable.

The theory had seemed attractive for a while. Bacterial spores, protected by a thick coat, are very resistant to cold and dehydration, and might conceivably last a long time in the vacuum of interstellar space. Also they are of just the right size to be more influenced by the outward pressure of a sun's radiation than by the inward pull of its gravity.

Again nudging Dr. Orgel toward his own theory, I put in another question. "Wasn't it Arrhenius who coined the word *panspermia* to describe his theory— the same word you've now adopted?"

"That's right. In the last ten or twenty years it's become more and more evident that neither his theory nor Lord Calvin's would work. A meteorite probably could never escape from another solar system. A spore coming from outer space would be destroyed long before it got here by the sun's ultraviolet light or other destructive radiations such as cosmic rays, solar X-rays, and zones of charged particles like the Van Allen belts around the Earth."

"Nevertheless, you think that panspermia was possible?" I asked. Our inverview was moving now to the heart of the mystery.

"Directed panspermia, as we call it, is a sort of last attempt to resurrect the theory that life could have come here from elsewhere," he said. "Our notion is that maybe life was deliberately sent here by a technological society on some other planet, probably in our own galaxy. It would have arrived in a rocket, in our opinion, if it arrived at all. ... Of course one is interested in any new evidence that might be relevant to this, and there are one or two slight fragments of evidence that are relevant."

He went on to explain some of the technical reasons why a seeding from outer space had suggested itself to him and to Crick. They had noticed that the element molybdenum was essential to animal life, important to plant life, and a vital part of many biochemical reactions. Yet molybdenum is a rare element—much less abundant on Earth than, say, chromium or nickel, which are relatively unimportant in life processes.

"The chemical composition of organisms must reflect to some extent the environment in which they evolved," Dr. Orgel said. To him this suggested that Earth life might have begun on a planet where molybdenum was plentiful.

"But the evidence that interests us most," he went on, "is the uniformity of all living systems on Earth today."

I understood what he meant. In spite of the present great diversity of living things, all have the same basic ground plan. Their cells all carry out metabolism in much the same way. There is only one genetic code for all terrestrial life. How could random chemical combinations all shape themselves into the same code?

"If life had arisen and evolved spontaneously here," he continued, "it seems at least possible that many very different forms of life would be competing with each other. But in fact we know that all living things have evolved from a single cell, which inhabited Earth about three or four billion years ago—and there don't seem to be any traces of any extinct competitors which arose in different ways. There are perfectly normal biological explanations of this that don't call for anything magical or anything extraterrestrial. But even when all is said and done, it remains a little surprising that there isn't any evidence for other sorts of organisms than the ones we see."

The implication was obvious. The first living cell, a single seed of protoplasm, a single microscopic organism, might have replicated itself billions and billions of times in short order. Its replicas would adjust to warmth or cold, evolving accordingly. In the course of time they would branch out along many different paths, and evolve as enzymes, genes, insulin, hemoglobin; they would organize into bone and muscles and organs and coordinate their work; they would begin the beating of hearts, the pumping of lungs, the vibrations of nerves, and ultimately, the flashes of thought. Dr. Orgel summed up for me:

"If life came from another planet, whether it came on a rocket or however it got here, we could understand very easily why there is only one sort of life. We would all be descendants from a single ancestor—the one that got here."

I asked, "If this happened, how long ago would it have happened?"

"We know that Earth was formed about four and a half billion years ago. We know that the earliest forms of life appeared more than three and a half billion years ago. So if our story were correct, we could say that life, however it got here, had to arrive between four and a half and three and a half billion years ago."

So there I had it, neatly laid out. Directed panspermia. The vision of thinking beings in some faraway world out beyond our solar system, launching a spacecraft carrying microorganisms such as dormant algae and bacterial spores, hurling it across the eternal void to arrive finally at Earth and sow the seeds of all future life.

I had asked for one hour of Dr. Orgel's time to film the interview. Forty-five minutes had passed. All I had managed to do was open a door through which I could glimpse a jumble of strange and wondrous possibilities.

I could have asked enough questions to fill another fifteen hours. These theoretical ancestors of ours on some remote planet, what sort of beings might they be? Obviously their civilization had to be more advanced than ours. Why would they plant seeds here? Could such seeding be merely the first step in a grand design for Earth—a design encompassing aeons?

But I was an interloper in this scientist's busy world. So we wrapped it up. Strolling toward his office, I asked a final question: "Do you believe that directed panspermia caused the origin of life on Earth?"

"No," he said. "It's just an interesting possibility." And then he left.


Going home to Los Angeles I felt a letdown. The interview had not given me any answers, just widened the scope of an investigation I had undertaken.

In 1972 I had produced a television special called "In Search of Ancient Astronauts." It had brought together on film some of the visible signs that Earth might have been visited long ago by astronauts from some other world—visitors whom the awed Earthmen would probably have taken for gods.

But that had been only a preliminary reconnaissance. Now I was committed to a more thorough quest.

My goal was to find evidence that a significant part of mankind's history could have been shaped by far-comers from another planet. Not final proof, of course—lifetimes of archaeological and geological probing might be needed to clinch the case—just an examination of unsolved historical mysteries that might all be solved by adducing certain extraterrestrial influences.

Months of shooting would be boiled down to fifty-one minutes and thirteen seconds of another television special to be called "In Search of Ancient Mysteries."

Timex was our sponsor, NBC our network, and all I had to do was scour the world for material.

When I had first outlined the project to my wife Sally, she remarked, "You make it sound like Earth was some student's field project in biology."

Well, maybe it was. Charles Fort, who spent a lifetime collecting evidence of phenomena that scientists couldn't explain, used to argue humorously:

"I think we're property. I should say we belong to something. I suspect that all this has been known, perhaps for ages, to certain ones upon this earth, a cult or order, members of which function like bellwethers to the rest of us, directing us in accordance with instructions received from somewhere."

The more Sally and I talked about the idea, the more questions she raised, the more deeply I was forced to dig into knowledge I had stored up during years of writing and producing films on nature and science.

In programs such as "The Undersea World of Jacques Cousteau," and the National Geographic Society specials, "How to Stay Alive" and "The New Explorers," I had dealt mainly with phenomena that could be found or induced almost on demand. With patience and some luck, I could photograph remarkable examples of life cycles, ecological balances, reactive patterns, and strange relationships; then I could go on to explain them in terms that audiences could understand. But in "Ancient Mysteries" there would be no provable explanations—just suppositions that would be possible explanations. The man in charge of programming for NBC, Larry White, said the program would be like "a quiz show without answers."

As we talked, I laid out for Sally some of the puzzles that might contain keys to a new explanation of man's past. Why does virtually every culture on Earth contain a legend of a great flood? Why do men so often think of their gods as looking down from high above? Where did ancient peoples suddenly acquire a vast knowledge of astronomy?

Soon my skeptical wife was hooked. So I got a first-rate partner in the "Ancient Mystery" undertaking. Writer, college English professor, repository of knowledge about classical myths, and one of the most resourceful researchers I ever met, she entered the search with me.

This book is the story of how we searched and what we found.

It is a product of significant assistance by others too. Beyond the scientists and assorted experts who gave willingly—but warily—of their time and knowledge, we found ourselves benefiting by many ideas of Fred Warshofsky, the field producer on the "Ancient Mystery" film.

But to speed the narrative, from here on I'll tell the story of our search from just one person's viewpoint—mine. Remember, as you read, that others were helping in many ways.

# II

## Spores and Artifacts

Musing about Dr. Orgel's spore rocket, I made a mental dive down through awesome depths of geologic time to imagine what Earth was like when—and if—the rocket came.

Perhaps three or four billion years ago Earth's infancy ended. Its raw crust became a metallic desert, a battlefield of the elements, lit by the lurid glare of lava fountains, rumbling and quivering from earthquakes. Was that how it looked when the rocket tumbled into the planet's gravitational pull?

For an instant a projectile would have streaked through the vapor, leaving a trail like a tracer bullet, then plunged into the warm sea or hit the solid rock with an impact that could have created one of the circular pits still visible at a few places on Earth's surface.

The container might have taken ten thousand years to break open. What matter? The particles within could lie dormant for untold ages. And Earth itself was in no hurry to mature.

When at last the specks of life emerged, they probably faced heavy odds against finding chemical nutrients to sustain them. Yet they did find some, if Dr. Orgel's surmise is valid. Possibly many packages were scattered over the planet from a rocket or orbiting spacecraft, and only one or two proved viable.

When and if they did, this was the moment when life began its mysterious ascension. From slime and

9

stardust, from one microscopic cell miraculously born and fertilized, came something that advanced to the writing of symphonies and the weighing of nebulas.

But think how long it took! Can you visualize the number of years in one billion-year period? Try this simple mental exercise. Make an estimate of how many minutes have passed since the day Christ was born.

Probably you guess the total to be in uncountable figures. Most people do. But even today, not many more than a billion minutes have gone by since Christ's birth.

If life began on Earth three and a half billion years ago, and if mankind has been a separate species here for the last two million years, as anthropologists believe, then the whole slow process of evolution from the first blob of jelly up to thinking human could have repeated itself more than two thousand times during the period the Earth has existed—and can be repeated many more thousands of times during the coming five billion years that Earth will presumably be habitable by man.

Sir James Jeans helps us visualize these time spans by asking us to imagine an obelisk the height of the Washington Monument, with a penny on top of it and a postage stamp lying on the penny. Proportionately the monument represents the age of Earth, the penny the whole age of mankind, and the stamp the length of time since men learned to use a piece of stone as a tool.

This puts in perspective a question that bothered me. What could the senders of the rocket hope to gain by planting a seed that would not come to harvest for such a gigantically long time?

Perhaps there was an answer in what astronomers saw when they searched the heavens. Up there are stars in all stages of evolution. There are faint blood-red dwarfs so cool that their surface temperature is a mere 4,000 degrees Fahrenheit. There are searing ghosts blazing at 100,000 degrees and almost too hot to be seen, for their radiation is mostly in the invisible ultraviolet.

Stars, like persons, go through vicissitudes and ultimately grow old. Our Sun will someday flare into a red giant, burning the surface of the Earth to crisp. Then it will dwindle down to the white-dwarf stage. It will be a tiny thing, not much bigger than Earth, and will radiate very little heat. The daylight on Earth will be as dim as moonlight, and the temperature will have fallen to 300 degrees below zero.

Many suns have already reached this phase, and others are in all stages of aging. Yet the intelligent life on a planet of such a sun wouldn't necessarily be doomed. It would simply have to move out to another solar system as its own sun began to burn. There would be ample warning. A migration to other planets should be child's play to the intelligence we might expect of a species after a few thousand centuries of civilization. Very far ahead of time, a highly advanced race might begin to prepare a new home for its descendants.

But could there be such a species close enough to reach us, I wondered, even in spaceships traveling at nearly the speed of light?

I asked Dr. Su Shu Huang, astronomy professor at Northwestern University, to assess the likelihood of life in solar systems near us.

"I'm very optimistic that life is elsewhere outside our solar system," he said. "I believe that mainly because of statistics. I found that all stars similar to our Sun are expected to have planetary systems."

"Why is this expected?" I pressed.

"Solar-type stars give off their energy in a moderate way, so that they last around ten billion years. Because they last this long, they're likely to support life. A sun must have a very long life-span in order to maintain life on any of its planets. We emerged on Earth because the Sun is very stable, radiating steadily for five billion years, and it will be radiating at the same rate another five billion."

"How many stars similar to the Sun are in our galaxy?"

"Just in our own so-called Milky Way system, there are more than a billion stars of this type. If all those stars have an average life of ten billion years, some life will appear on the planets. Once life appears, it will go up and up very naturally. So we have no reason to believe that it should not be highly intelligent."

I remembered when planets were regarded as the results of cosmic accidents that could occur only a very few times. But astronomers' knowledge has broadened in the past thirty years, convincing them that many if not most stars hold planets in orbit. In 1942 a planet was seen within the double-star system 61 Cygni, one of our neighbors. It would be a fantastic coincidence, if planets truly were rare, to find one practically in our backyard.

The seven thousand stars seen by my unaided eyes, plus tens of thousands of others visible only to telescopes, are all part of our tremendous whirlpool galaxy, the Milky Way. The oldest stars in this galaxy are much older than our Sun. One astronomer's estimate was eight billion years. The famous Swiss-American astronomer Fritz Zwicky speculated on ages as great as a million billion years.

Our Sun is a very ordinary star—a yellow dwarf, midway between the largest and the smallest, and between the hottest blue stars and the coolest red giants. Su Shu Huang believed that a billion stars in the galaxy must be very similar to the Sun. I delved into astronomy books for additional opinions about the likelihood that they possessed planets similar to Earth.

Within "our" galaxy, according to the estimates of Dr. Carl Sagan, one planet in each two thousand or so must be almost a duplicate of Earth. On it we might well step out of a space vehicle, take a deep breath of oxygen-rich air, look up at a blue sky, and jump or run with about the same ease (i.e., gravitational pull) that we feel here.

If indeed one two-thousandth of the planets in this galaxy are habitable by life as we know it, and if life has indeed evolved there by the same rules and time scale that govern Earth life, then Dr. Sagan would guess there are a minimum of fifty thousand civilizations more intelligent than ours. It seemed like an awful lot of people out there—until I remembered that there are a hundred billion stars in our galaxy.

I looked up another estimate. Space scientist Stephen H. Dole made a detailed study of the possibilities in his book *Habitable Planets for Man*, published in 1964. He calculated the chances that a star of the right size might have a planet of the right mass, at the right distance, in an appropriate orbit, spinning at about the right speed. By making what seemed to him conservative estimates, he concluded that there were likely to be 600 million habitable planets in the galaxy, each of them already generating some forms of life.

If these habitable planets were spread more or less evenly throughout the galaxy, Dole estimated that the nearest to us should be some twenty-seven light years away, and that within a hundred light years of Earth there should be a total of fifty habitable planets.

This might be close enough for one of them to shoot spore-carrying rockets at us. But was it close enough for a mass migration of living beings? Possibly it was—if they could be put into suspended animation for a few centuries, and could be reawakened when they reached the vicinity of Earth.

One important note must be made here. Time stretches during space travel, so that cosmonauts live much longer, although they aren't aware of doing so. This astounding fact was predicted by Einstein's equations in his relativity theory, and was later verified experimentally, just as other parts of his theory were. The lifetimes of fast-moving unstable cosmic-ray particles called muons were precisely measured in space, and in every case their lives lengthened as their speed in space increased. For them, "time" slowed down. For the same reason, if you were on a spacecraft, you might age only a few years while people on Earth lived a whole lifetime.

Anyhow, getting back to Dole's calculations, I found that his later observations improved the probabilities of life near us. He counted fourteen stars of the right type within twenty-two light years of Earth. The highest likelihood of habitable planets, he found, were in the two stars closest to us, the sunlike Alpha Centauri A and B, less than five light years away. These two stars, taken together, had one chance in ten of possessing habitable planets, Dole estimated. The total probability for all fourteen was about two chances in five.

In the galaxy as a whole, if intelligent life were flourishing on one of every two thousand habitable planets, it would mean there might be three hundred thousand civilizations. We could be far from alone in our galaxy.

At least one in each thousand of those civilizations presumably measured its age not in thousands but in millions of years. This would seem almost inevitable, if Earth truly were one of the younger of the habitable planets. Our species has existed only during the last seven-thousandth of Earth's history. Such extreme youth on any cosmic time scale would make it likely that hundreds of other-worldly civilizations must be superior to us by aeons of development.

Only science-fiction writers used to take such possibilities seriously. But I knew that by the 1970s nearly all astronomers accepted the high probability of intelligent life on many planets. U.S. scientists set up an enterprise called Project Ozma to listen for possible radio signals from other worlds. Later Project Cyclops, involving more than twenty experts in a variety of fields, began feasibility studies of other ways to detect intelligent life in nearby solar systems.

A 1972 report by a committee of the National Academy of Sciences said, "At this instant, through this very document, are perhaps passing radio waves bearing the conversations of distant creatures, conversations that we could record if we but pointed a radio telescope in the right direction and tuned to the proper frequency."

Theoretically we could pick up two kinds of signals: those sent intentionally by civilizations seeking to make themselves known, and those sent inadvertently by civilizations that have radio and television transmissions like our own. In either case, experts could distinguish such signals from the random emissions of natural radio sources.

I found that Russian astronomers were already eavesdropping on about fifty nearby stars. And as early as 1963 they began to zero in on two radio sources in particular, the signals coming from the vicinity of stars catalogued by the California Institute of Technology under the names CTA-21 and CTA-102 (one in the constellation Aries, the other in Pegasus). What made these sources remarkable was that the wavelength range of their signals was in the ten to fifty centimeter range. Brainy broadcasters would choose this very range as ideal for purposes of interplanetary communication, because such waves would be least likely to meet interference or distortion on long voyages and wouldn't be masked by radio waves of nonintelligent origin, which go out on much longer wavelengths.

In 1964 a leading Soviet astronomer, Nikolai S. Kardashev, boldly suggested that these radio waves were probably sent out by a supercivilization far in advance of us. Why did he think so? Because the intensity of the signals was well beyond our own capacity to match.

Wherever I turned I found affirmation for the idea of intelligent life existing elsewhere in the universe. One critical question, however, kept popping up. All the research was pointing me toward looking for a reason why Dr. Orgel's spore-carrying rocket might have been targeted for Earth. The National Aeronautics and Space Administrations report on Project Cyclops gave me an interesting kernel to consider. In part it reads:

> Today man faces a new threat as the dominant species of this planet. In Pogo's words, "We have met the enemy and he is us." Man must either sublimate the basic drive of uninhibited growth, converting it into a quest for quality rather than quantity, and assume responsibility for the husbandry of the planet he dominates or die a cultural failure killing his own kind.

We are almost surely not the first culture in the Galaxy to face this problem; in fact, it would appear that our present situation is the direct result of technological mastery over our environment and would therefore confront all life forms at our stage of development.

The implication I read into the report startled me. It seemed to say that having reached the point where it was strangling on its own technology, a civilization in some distant galaxy might have sent off a life-raft rocket.

Other scenarios were possible. One planet might have been spraying all the nearer solar systems with spore-carrying rockets, say once every hundred thousand years or so, as a sort of gift to posterity or just as an experiment, to see what would happen.

If this really were an experiment, the planners doubtless would want to check back periodically on the results. Duncan Lunan thought so, and produced some rather unusual evidence to back his idea. An intense, bearded young Scotsman, Lunan is a fellow of the British Interplanetary Society. He started his explanation by playing a simulated series of signals that had been transmitted into space more than forty-five years ago. After the first signal went out, it echoed back to Earth, bearing a new pattern. Here's how he explained it to me:

"In 1927 there were recorded for the first time certain long-delayed radio echoes. What was happening was that signals were being sent out on an experimental basis to test for natural echoes within the Earth's atmosphere and echoes passing around the world and effects of this kind. Oslo reported some very peculiar echoes at certain times of the year, which were apparently coming from the distance of the moon."

I asked if they understood the echoes to be signals. "No, the experimenters at the time felt sure they were dealing with some kind of natural reflection or radio waves from out in space. They began to conduct a series of experiments and eventually they increased the separation of their pulses. When they were then sending out pulses twenty seconds apart, something very strange happened. The echoes stopped for a couple of weeks, then they returned as before on the thirty-three-seconds delay. But after ten minutes, they began to vary and I've got here the record of one such sequence that was recorded."

I was drawn into Lunan's net. "What you're saying is that the signals had special meaning."

"The interpretation that I put forward here," he responded, "rests on the assumption that the echoes come from a space probe." He explained the origin of the space probe based on a complex mathematical interpretation of the pattern of signals returning to Earth. He traced it to the Constellation of Boötis, showing how the bleeps of signal translate to star map coordinates. He pointed on his map to one of the stars and continued.

"What has happened is that the star has exhausted the reserves of hydrogen in its core, as all stars do eventually. It is now in a phase in which its core is contracting, its outer atmosphere is expanding, and it's putting out very much more heat during this period, a matter of millions of years rather than thousands of millions. Any intelligent life in such a planetary system would, therefore, find itself in the situation of having to get away, firstly, to the outer planets of the system and in the longer term, to leave the system altogether and to escape to some planet of some other star. Therefore, the space probes are sent out to locate habitable planets."

Without relating to one another, two different parts of the world with entirely different fields of expertise were adding random items to my list of questions. Dr. Orgel's spore rocket, Duncan Lunan's habitation-seeking probe had been added to my list of possibilities. There were others to be considered.

Suppose a mighty mother ship, a mechanized island community of some kind, lay waiting among the cold outer giants of the Sun's scattered family? Would it not send vehicles to Earth from time to time?

Suddenly I remembered oddities I had come across in astronomy books. Nobody knows why little Phobos, the inner moon of Mars only ten miles across, registers on our instruments as being a thousand times lighter than that much water would be; if the figure is correct, Phobos must be a hollow shell, which led Dr. I. S. Shlovskii, an eminent Soviet mathematician, to speculate that it might be an artificial satellite parked in orbit by space explorers. Nor can we be sure that the innermost of Jupiter's twelve satellites isn't a giant spacecraft put there by somebody sometime. It has an odd habit of disappearing and reappearing at unpredictable intervals, and of altering its orbit.

Whatever the scenario, if some other society had been in contact with Earth—had seen something of value here—then by all logic it would try to keep in contact. And it might still be sending observers here occasionally.

I remembered the U.S. Air Force's study of unidentified flying objects, which it summarized in 1969. The air force had thoroughly investigated the reports of 2,199 sightings. It found that most could be explained as optical illusions, weather balloons, swamp gas, balls of electricity, or other fairly normal occurrences. But there were 440 sightings, each by a number of witnesses, that it couldn't explain by any hypothesis whatever. Perhaps to hide its embarrassment, it summarily closed the investigation.

September was the peak month for sightings—another inexplicable fact, since it kept recurring.

When I learned of a sighting on Labor Day eve, 1973, by a Georgia state trooper, I determined to get an interview. State troopers are in their own realistic way trained reporters.

The officer's name was Walter Caldwell. The morning after his experience in Manchester, Georgia, he gave this account:

"It was last night around eleven o'clock. I was standing outside my car when a light came across the sky and just stopped up in the air. There was a straight beam of light coming out of the bottom of it. It would sit perfectly still and then it would take off real fast and stop, then make a ninety-degree turn—

four ninety-degree turns—and come back to the very spot where it started from. I didn't jump to any conclusion. I called on the radio and got another state trooper, and he came while I was there and he saw the same thing."

"Were there other witnesses?" the interviewer asked.

"I got the city police out of Pine Mountain, the city police out of Warm Springs. Two state troopers out of La Grange came down. We stayed and watched this thing for about two hours and a half."

"How far away from it were you?"

"I would say four or five miles—just guessing."

"How high in the sky do you figure it was?"

"It was about a forty-five degree angle off the ground. We could see a blue light on top of it, and then when it turned, we could see two blue lights on each side of it."

"You say each side of it?"

"Well, it was round-looking," Caldwell elaborated, "except for that one beam of light that came out of the bottom, and it looked like there might have been something under there, but I couldn't make it out."

"When you say 'something under there,' are you saying that the beam of light came out and radiated around a darker object, which was at the base of whatever you saw?"

"It looked like it might be some arms or something coming out of the bottom. I've never seen anything like it. Some people asked me, Was it a flying saucer, but I've never seen a flying saucer. I've never seen anything like this either."

There had been accounts of strange moving lights in the sky, strange objects by daylight, reported in newspapers of the nineteenth century, long before anyone invented the term *flying saucer*. Unless one disbelieved all the reports, one had to admit the possibility that spacecraft might have darted in and out of our atmosphere many times. A vast amount has been written on both sides of the question. But very little dealt with why they might have come.

A coherent theory of why they came, and when,

and how often, might sketch out a new story of mankind—a longer and stranger story than conventional historians would consider. The story might indicate that everyone on Earth was descended from a race elsewhere in the galaxy. I was beginning to sense the dim outlines of a theory of my own.

Was there any evidence to support my hypothesis? At least I knew of numerous inexplicable discoveries reported in the annals of various technical societies—reported and then ignored.

The flood of new information in all fields of enterprise has become so overwhelming in the past three decades that researchers have had to concentrate closely on their own narrow specialties. Discoveries that don't fit an established framework of knowledge are likely to be hurriedly forgotten.

Nevertheless, enigmatic findings have been made. Here is a brief catalog of what I came to call Ancient Mysteries.

Louis Pauwels and Jacques Bergier reported that ancient ornaments were discovered on an Andean plateau by anthropologist J. Alden Mason. The ornaments were formed from molten platinum. Platinum's melting point is 1,730 degrees. There is no evidence that any ancient people had blast furnaces or any other equipment capable of generating such heat.

The same researchers mention the uncovering of an object made of aluminum alloy in a tomb sixteen centuries old. The only known method of extracting aluminum from bauxite ore is electrolysis, devised by Faraday in 1808.

Filming in Colombia, I found a strange gold object. It was a clear model of a delta-winged jet fighter, and it was thought to be two thousand years old. Ivan Sanderson, a former British Naval Intelligence officer, mentioned a manufactured gold chain found in a Pennsylvania coal deposit at least a million years old.

The *Proceedings of the Royal Irish Academy* for October, 1852, discussed the finding by various people of some sixty cubes "sown broadcast over the country in some strange way that I cannot offer solution of," according to a Dr. Frazer who examined them. The inscriptions on them are said to be "a very ancient class of Chinese characters." Archaeologists are unanimous that ancient China had no known link with Ireland.

In the Mojave Desert, in prehistoric rock strata, the print of a sandal was uncovered. It appeared to have been manufactured rather than handmade.

In 1900, divers off the coast of Greece brought up a hunk of ancient corroded bronze. When archaeologists carefully cleaned and examined it, they found it was a highly complicated mechanism with more than twenty gears turning dials that gave amazingly complete astronomical information about the rising, setting, and courses of various stars. Inscriptions on its surface, giving instructions for its use, are early Greek. The Greeks of antiquity were not known to possess machinery of any kind.

From La Venta, Mexico, came reports of ancient concave mirrors. The Bureau of American Ethnology at the Smithsonian Institution said they are very skillfully made to give effects almost identical with the modern practice of parabolizing optical reflectors. No one has any idea how the ancient Mexicans made them, or used them.

In 1968, geologist Korium Megertchain found evidence in Armenia of a metallurgical industry where gloved workers used steel tweezers and wore protective mouth filters, implying they handled delicate miniaturized assemblies. The artifacts have been dated at about 3000 B.C.

Long before the existence of telescopes, the Tower of the Winds in Athens contained a model of the universe and a complex clock. It was built in 50 B.C. by a Macedonian astronomer, Andronikos of Kyrrhos.

In the British Museum are cuneiform tablets from Babylon. They describe the location of an outer planet that could not be known without telescopes. Galileo has always been thought to have invented the first telescope—centuries after Babylon.

In Delhi I filmed an iron tower that is at least fifteen hundred years old yet shows no signs of rust.

Rust-proof ferrous metals have only recently been alloyed.

They were no less startling than the quartz beads taken from a mummy in Cuzco, Peru. The beads had very tiny holes drilled in them. I was told that only recently have we developed a commercial drill to make such holes.

Each of these anomalies was a mystery in itself, but a dead-end mystery. There was no way to investigate it further. I couldn't make a television documentary merely by displaying these inanimate curios.

But I had heard of much bigger mysteries in certain parts of the world—mysteries involving whole dead civilizations. Within their ruins I might find facts that would fit together to account for all those strange artifacts—and that would perhaps help me follow a faint trail of preternaturally intelligent beings of long ago.

These were the mysteries I must investigate.

# III

## *The Sea in the Mountains*

And so I set out. I was infected by detectivitis.

Archaeology is one of the least heralded sports in the world: a healthy outdoor game, with all the suspense and challenge of a mystery story. It's generally played by an ingroup of professionals. First an enigma appears. A splendid culture has died while apparently in good health. You find the corpus delicti: silent old ruins. You find a mass of detail that would tantalize any sleuth: the testimony of carved stones, scraps of cloth and pottery, writings in code, buried skeletons, hearsay handed down through generations.

To make it more intriguing, clues have been confused, misread, and lost by blundering strangers before the first detective arrived. If you try to reconstruct what happened, you need the patience of a jigsaw-puzzle addict who also likes riddles. You should be young enough to take strenuous trips into strange places, and perhaps to be challenged as a suspicious character yourself. If you are all this, you'll have an exciting time, and go home to be hailed as either a great expert or a fool.

I began my sleuthing quietly in libraries. Scholars and diggers had been at work for a century on mysteries of dead cities all around the globe. I wanted to be familiar with their findings.

As I read, day after day, I began to see a supreme

mystery underlying all the others. The ultimate mystery wasn't how and why the ancient civilizations died, but how they were born. Where had they come from in the first place? Had they really evolved with the infinite slowness that the conventional professors postulated?

The standard prosaic explanations seemed to paper over a multitude of weak spots. There were facts that didn't fit. In the back of my own mind, a far-out surmise took shape. Weird as it was, nothing in the books nullified it.

Here and there a well-developed culture had appeared rather suddenly, almost like an explosion. Could civilizations have sprung from some magic seed, planted far back before the counting of years began?

If so, I thought I knew where it might have happened.

There is a place where Mother Nature is not moderate. The mountains are huge and the sun is dangerous, and the freezing dark comes bang on the heels of day. In reading the authorities' books I had noted certain facts that pointed me toward that place.

I'll tell you about the facts as we go along. Fly to Peru with me.

No other country of the world resembles Peru in physical features. Black beaches and the wash of giant seas on a coastal desert where rain almost never falls. Great mountains marching down the world, to dwarf a man's images of his own importance. Among these mountains, between two principal ranges, there is a vast plateau in the sky where cloud-seas flow below you while the sun burns you through icy air.

It is called the Altiplano—the High Plain, more than two miles high—and it lies athwart the invisible border between Peru and Bolivia. Some people call it the Roof of the World. It is slightly higher than Lhasa in Tibet.

In the flattest northern reaches of this bleak windswept waste is an inland sea, Lake Titicaca, which is sometimes described as "the most remarkable body of water in the world."

What is remarkable about it? To begin with, it is the world's highest navigable lake, 12,507 feet above sea level. And it is so big that when you stand on a rocky hill at one edge and look to the horizon, the land is hidden below the edge of the world. You see only water, as if it were an ocean. It is 122 miles long, as wide as 35 miles in some places, brimming across 3,200 square miles. The water is fresh—and paralyzingly cold.

I knew of Lake Titicaca from work I had done producing an episode in "The Undersea World of Jacques Cousteau" television series. When I finally made the trip to the lake, I realized how hostile the environment was. As soon as I stepped out onto the Altiplano my heart raced, blood pounded in my ears, I felt unpleasantly light-headed—as if gravity itself had weakened—and the dry rarefied air burned my nose and throat.

Life seemed alien to the place. Nothing was easy for us. Candles wouldn't burn brightly in the oxygen-poor atmosphere. Campfires weren't hot. Water boiled at only 189 degrees so that cooking a soft-boiled egg took twice as long as down on the coast.

If we put the normal amount of leavening in bread dough, it inflated like a balloon; air pressure was only eight pounds per square inch compared to fifteen pounds at sea level. Engines were hard to start, and they lost a third of their rated horsepower. Aircraft needed a two-mile run to get airborne. Seeds wouldn't sprout in the barren soil. There were tales that no white woman had ever given birth on the Altiplano.

We never really adjusted to its hostile climate. We had nausea. Headaches. I sweated in the sun, but there was a deadly cold and continual flutter of air in my ears; I shivered in the heat. My high blue daze gave me eerie imaginings that this was a land of sealed buried sorcerers, of miracles lost in time.

Cousteau's divers judged the lake to be at least seven hundred feet deep. They didn't find the sunken Inca gold we had visualized, and the films they brought back were a disappointment at the time.

Cousteau said, "If only we'd taken advantage of the archaeology story—" but I cut him off.

"Jacques, that's just stones and bones," I said. "The audience wants fish, underwater romance." It wasn't until I returned to the study of Lake Titicaca years later that I knew what he meant.

Peruvian Indians dominate the resident population. No one lives near the lake but Indians. They seem shy, dour people to us. Their faces are hairless. In all the Andes no Indian has hair on his face today. But before recorded time their ancestors built monuments to bearded prophets.

For decades now, explorers have gone in to question these Indians—spectacled white men of this new hybrid race we call Caucasian, trying to read the story of the past; but the natives only stare at them and give vague replies. On the Altiplano they speak a language called Aymara—which brings us to one of the most remarkable facts about Lake Titicaca.

In the Aymara tongue, Titicaca means literally "stone of the jaguar."

Why had a cat been chosen as the name of this frigid sea?

Scholars answered briskly, "A jaguar god was worshiped at many places in the mountains before the Incas came. The lake was probably a ceremonial center."

It is true that scattered through Peru are tall stone idols with the fanged grin of a jungle cat. Jaguar or puma faces have been found painted on pottery and woven into textiles, some that were old a thousand years before Christ. Most authorities agree that Peru's first true civilization was associated with the appearance of a jaguar god. This god was a symbol of supernatural strength and wisdom whose cult spread from valley to valley among the steep mountains and down to the sea and the eastern jungle.

Still I wondered. Why a jaguar?

One answer came from a totally unexpected source: U.S. astronauts. Orbiting the earth from 170 miles up, they photographed Titicaca.

When an archaeologist who knew that area saw the pictures, he pointed. "I see the jaguar!"

The outline of the main lake, as seen from outer space, resembled a bas-relief of a jaguar, with outstretched claws and open jaws, pouncing at a fleeting rabbit (a smaller body of water adjacent to it).

The lost race who came before the Incas could never have seen Lake Titicaca from space—could they?

Maybe there was some more mundane reason to give the lake its peculiar name. Maybe it was just a place to go and meditate about their god, although I found no stone likenesses of him.

But I knew I wanted to follow the faint clues to these shadowy people. Who were they? I ran after them down the infinite corridors of time.

When the Spanish ex-swineherd Francisco Pizarro and his handful of adventurers reached Peru in 1532, they found the most far-flung and highly organized civilization of its time: the great Inca commonwealth of six million people.

They also noticed many abandoned ruins.

Ridges were edged with battlements built by unknown hands. In the dizzy heights of what is now Bolivia, called Upper Peru by the Spaniards, stood ruins of great stone buildings whose architects were enigmas even to the educated Incas. They could only tell their conquerors that these structures had been created by some nameless race long ago—or perhaps by giants or gods.

Spanish chroniclers of the sixteenth and seventeenth centuries were helpful to modern researchers, for they wrote voluminously, reporting what they saw and heard, gathering up every wisp of oral history. There was no written history. The Incas, in spite of their talent for government, had not invented any kind of writing except a complex shorthand of many-colored knots in strings, comprehensible only to the "rememberers" who kept them, and indecipherable after the rememberers died.

This device was called a quipu. The more I learned about it, the more I wondered if the Incas or their predecessors got the idea from seeing a computer used by visitors from another planet. The quipu was (among other things) a mathematical tool that might be called a homemade computer.

The whole Inca civilization depended on it, in a way. This great nation had no other system of keeping records, nor of solving mathematical problems.

When Inca engineers planned their buildings or highways or irrigation works, they couldn't write any names or numbers on their maps, couldn't label their parts, couldn't consult handbooks to determine how thick the cables of a suspension bridge should be. Their records were kept on quipus, and their mathematical computations were done on quipus.

A quipu was a cord about two feet long, composed of different colored strings tightly twisted together, from which smaller strings were suspended like a fringe. Instead of engraving something on a tablet or writing it on paper, the Incas simply tied knots in these strings. The knots stood for numerals when the quipu served as a computer. The number of loops in the knot expressed the digits from one to nine, and zero was indicated by a gap. In ways not very well understood now, the Incas used the quipu to work out problems very quickly, with accuracy that amazed the Spaniards.

Instead of the twenty-number system of the Mayans (who were unknown in Peru), the Andean peoples used a decimal system. To do this, you need the idea expressed by our word *digit*—and you also need the idea, much more abstract and sophisticated, which we express by the concept zero. Finally you must have thought out the idea of place value. Whoever invented the quipu was a man of mighty brainpower.

Charles V, king of Spain and Holy Roman emperor, didn't know and couldn't have found out the number of people in Spain, the weight and worth of his harvests, or any other rudimentary social statistic. But each Inca territorial governor knew from his quipus exactly how many people he governed, how many were qualified to bear arms, how many were females, what volume of all crops had been produced that season and where, what stores were available in warehouses, how many casualties were suffered in the last campaign, and how many of the enemy had been killed.

Each year the skeins of many-colored strings were forwarded to the capital, where they constituted what we could call the national census, national archives, internal revenue service, and various other national bureaus. No wonder that Inca military campaigns were constantly successful. And no wonder that ignorant and superstitious Spanish friars were amazed at what the natives could do with their quipus.

As an information-retrieval system (another way in which modern computers are used), a quipu was equally surprising. The worthy priest Morua tells how he met an old Inca who produced a quipu and, by fingering its knots, used it to repeat to the priest the whole Christian calendar with all its feasts and vigils; he had made it years before while listening to a friar.

Thus, the quipu could be either a system of numerical notation and computation, or a mnemonic device and a record of every fact that the Inca wanted to refer to. For an illiterate people, the device was almost unbelievably advanced. I had the feeling that their ancient white god had given someone the system.

Because the Incas had risen to importance less than a century before the Spaniards overthrew them, their traditions shed no light on Peru's remote past. The legends among older peoples, which might have told more, were systematically stamped out by the Inca satraps as they made themselves masters of the Andes. Therefore, the piecing together of Peru's prehistory depends on combinations of science and guesswork.

Scientists know that men lived in the Andes at least eleven thousand years ago. Probably a good deal earlier. They were primitive hunters, the standard books said.

Well, probably. But I couldn't imagine where they got the skills and knowledge to create the impressive heritage they left. And I found that some of the great experts wondered too.

Archaeologists Julip C. Tello and Rafael Larco

Hoyle of Peru, working with Professor Wendell C. Bennett of Yale University, made finds in 1940 that convinced them that civilized people had spread across a wide patch of northern and central Peru. When? At a very rough guess, two thousand years before the Incas.

At some period, those pre-Inca mountaineers dug great networks of irrigation canals. They used fertilizers to enrich crops. They understood smelting, welding, and soldering. They wove brocades, gauze, and tapestries.

You should see their tapestry. It sometimes has as many as five-hundred two-ply woolen strands to the inch. The best European tapestry before the power loom contains no more than one hundred.

More startling yet, a large number of skulls show that the owners, when alive, underwent and recovered from trepanning operations. No archaeologist has thought of any plausible explanation for this. Had prehistoric Peruvians already discovered that prefrontal lobotomy could cure some mental disorders? Anyhow, they left proofs of astounding surgical skill with bronze scalpels.

If you doubt me, listen to Dr. Roy L. Moodie in his *Studies in Paleopathology*: "No primitive or ancient race anywhere in the world had developed such surgical knowledge as had the pre-Columbian Peruvians. Their surgical attempts include amputations, excisions, bone transplants, cauterizations, and other less evident procedures."

To my mind, just possibly they had electronic devices too.

Gold is a very good electrical conductor. Gold ear coverings were worn by Incas of the highest rank, and by nobody else. The Spaniards called them Orejón, the "long ears." Could the earpieces have been receivers? Or could they have been connected to wires implanted in their brains?

Such implantations are used today to control epileptic seizures; to enable an alcoholic to overcome his weakness by pressing a button that "turns off" his desire to drink whenever he feels it coming on;

and—in experimental monkeys—to give themselves highly pleasurable sensations.

If the Incas knew some way to enhance their health or intelligence by wiring themselves, the gold ear-pieces would conceal the wiring. Otherwise, those cumbersome metal earmuffs would be a nuisance. Historians have strained hard to think of an explanation. Their reasoning is that the first Inca to wear these coverings must have done so to hide the fact that he'd lost an ear in battle, and the rest of his court emulated him. Maybe.

It would be interesting to have an electronics specialist examine those gold earpieces, which are abundantly available. They were found on mummies in numerous Inca graves.

Over a long period of time (dates unknown) the pre-Columbian Peruvians built mountain cities. Where else in the world have mountain peoples been urbanites? The terrain makes large-scale construction very difficult. Besides, the basic struggle to exist at all on the heights uses up energy. Nevertheless, there were cities clinging precariously to the flanks of colossal rock slopes in the high Andes. And these cities didn't just grow, as most ancient and modern cities did. These were planned from the beginning: terraces and irrigation systems and regular blocks of streets within massive walls. One city covered eleven square miles. No city in Europe or the U.S. was that big until the nineteenth century.

Of all the immense silent stone structures in the Andes, to me the most mystifying was Ollantaytambo, a pre-Incan fortress. It was mystifying because there seemingly was no way it could have been built.

Its rock walls were tightly fitted blocks weighing twelve tons or more. Each block must have been brought from a mountaintop quarry seven miles away. This meant moving them somehow across a hideous rent in the mountain chain—down several thousand feet, then up again.

At the bottom of this awful chasm the blocks had to

be taken across a torrent in which boulders danced
along like pebbles. It could not be bridged, because
the rock walls were sheer on each side. Maybe the
engineers managed to dam half the cataract at a
time, so that it could be diverted around the blocks as
they were inched across, as if they moved through
locks in a canal, so to speak.

Even so, there was no visible way to boost the
blocks to towering heights. The only paths were
threadlike ones worn by surefooted llamas.

Andean city builders, whoever they were, didn't
glorify kings or chiefs. The public works served the
people's welfare. There were no rich men owning
slaves, no rich organizations ruling sharecroppers.
Money, being uncalled for, was not invented.

Decade after decade archaeologists keep digging,
weighing and measuring, groping for new clues to the
vanished people who colonized the Andes for unreck-
oned centuries before the Inca conquest. The more
they discovered, the less certain they became of what
they knew. A 1964 report by Alfred Kidder II, eminent authority at the University of Pennsylvania, admitted: "Many chapters of man's history in Latin
America remain a blank. . . . Cotton that can be spun
poses a problem of origin that is still unsolved. . . .
The development of pottery, carbon-dated to around
1500 B.C., for the most part remains a mystery. . . .
The question of whether man in ancient America
evolved his own culture or imported it has inspired
many a wild surmise."

I'd like to make a wild surmise of my own. Will
you join me in a flight of fancy?

Assume that you and I are astronauts, not from
Earth, but from one of the other thousands of habitable planets calculated to exist in our galaxy.

Long ago we were launched from our planet, while
a robot set our course. After we escaped from orbit,
we lay on our padded couches and waited for the machines to take charge. We never heard the first whis-
per of gas as we fell asleep.

The air crept hissing from our capsule, and its heat

drained out into the ultimate cold of space. No decay could enter here; we lay in a tomb that would outlast any ever built on our planet, and might indeed outlast the planet itself. But it was more than a tomb, for its machines bided their time, and every hundred years a circuit opened and closed, counting the centuries.

So we slept in the cosmos beyond reach of our sun. On the world we had left, cities crumbled, mountains slid down, seas shrank. Ice crawled and spread from the poles as our sun cooled. We knew nothing of this, though probably we had foreseen it.

The centuries lengthened into a millennium, perhaps, and the millennia into aeons. But suddenly, at last, our magnificent ship remembers commands given it so long ago.

It chooses a path toward a star that fits certain specifications programmed into its miniaturized brain. Out of millions of possible solar systems, it has happened to select the sun that warms the planet Earth.

It does not check speed until it is among the inner planets. Here it begins its search, in the temperate zone where Mars and Venus and Earth circle. It presently recognizes a planet of the kind it seeks. It veers into orbit around Earth.

For a while the robot searches through its electronic memories and considers the situation. Then it makes its decision. If a robot could shrug its shoulders, it would do so. We can always turn away and search elsewhere, if this planet doesn't fill the bill, it might be reminding us.

It slowly warms us, responding to signals from its external sensors. Are you still with me? You and I lie for a while in a daze, knowing that we exist but not knowing who we are or whence we came. Then memory returns. We stir with excitement. The curiosity that has sent us across an abyss may soon be rewarded.

Fully awake now, we look down and study this new world that has been singled out for evaluation. Its size is correct: about the size of the home-world we left. It has the necessary oceans, land masses, atmosphere. We circle closer as our telemetry studies it in more detail.

Chemical properties of its atmosphere coincide with those we knew. Is it inhabited? Tests for carbon-based life-forms are positive.

Will it be warm enough for us, yet not too warm? The temperature spectrum looks tolerable in several parts of the globe.

Is the ground quaking? Apparently not much. Its electromagnetic emanations indicate faint quivering here and there, but the levels of activity are stable. That's reassuring.

Relative gravity? Equal in force to our own.

One difficulty is that cloud blankets obscure the land. But we make a dozen or more orbits, at different perigees and apogees. What we see looks good enough to justify on-site inspection.

So we skim around at lower altitude. We get ready to release packs of guidance instruments and pathfinder devices, programmed to find deep water for soft splashdowns.

We are looking for a large body of water near a flat open plain. The higher the better. We prefer thin clear atmosphere, to minimize dangers from infection or from any noxious gases, and to enable our ship to soak up energy from strong solar radiation.

Our computer makes the final selection for the test drop. It might have programmed one site that would match up, in a rudimentary way, with the area around the puma-shaped lake.

And so, on that great bleak steppe, you and I can finish our flight of fancy. We can land. Or at the very least we can drop seeds with the genetic code to become *Homo sapiens,* and then we can cruise off again, perhaps to return at intervals and inspect the crop we planted.

Fantasy? Of course. There is only the barest possibility that this is what really happened. But several peculiar events did occur at Lake Titicaca, ages ago. The evidence is still there.

Near the lake are beautiful round "burial places" of

stone, dating back centuries before the Inca era. Other miscellaneous artifacts have been found. There is no doubt that the lakeshore was inhabited, although the whole region is far from self-sufficient.

Conceivably the great jaguar cult started here. Conceivably it took a jaguar as its symbol in fond remembrance of the shape of the lake its founders saw when they came down from the heavens.

Nobody is sure where this strange potent religion started, or when. Some think it started in Mexico, because the pre-Aztec Olmecs worshiped a jaguar god too. Some think it was born on the edge of the Amazon jungle, where jaguars are plentiful, and then irresistibly climbed the Andes. Others say it could have been cradled at Titicaca.

Anyhow, it died out rather abruptly for unknown reasons, probably around 500 B.C., give or take a few centuries. But Peruvian civilization didn't die with the jaguar cult. It merely broke into fragments, each isolated, each developing in its own way.

Long afterward, a new religion arose. It became the first to include nearly all Peru. And where did it start? On this same bleak empty Altiplano, perhaps at a place ten miles from Lake Titicaca.

Inca legends told of its start. Some tales say that onto that wide stretch of water came gods—or a great shining light, in other versions—that brought forth two children who went down to found the Inca capital in the fertile Valley of Cuzco. To commemorate their birthplace, the Incas built terraces on an island in the lake. The terraces are still there, rising like a gigantic flight of stairs—and at the top of the stairs they put a stone temple called the House of the Incas. I saw its ruins, and pondered how two children could have come forth on the island.

To the Incas, this was the supreme place of their empire. They named it the Island of the Sun. The Inca royal family was believed descended from the sun.

I wanted to delve deeper into Incan mythology. I turned back to what was written by Pedro de Cieza de Leon in 1553: "These Indians say that their ancient ones hold it to be truth that there rose from this island of Titicaca a resplendent sun. For this reason they hold the isle to be a sacred place, building there a temple in honor of the sun."

Could the sun that rose so resplendently have been a departing spacecraft?

I explored still further. Garcilaso de la Vega was a primary source. His father was a Spaniard, his mother an Incan princess. Here are the recollections of his Incan uncle, told to de la Vega as a boy:

> Know that in ancient times the people lived like brute beasts without religion nor government, nor towns, nor houses.
>
> Our Father the Sun, seeing the human race in the condition I have described, sent down to earth a son and daughter to instruct them.
>
> With these commands our Father placed his two children in the lake of Titicaca: "I do good to the whole world, giving light that men may see, making them warm. You shall imitate this example as my children, sent to earth solely for the instruction and benefit of these men who live like beasts; and from this time I name you as lords, that you may instruct them."

Two questions stand out. First, what inspired the story? Second, why was the setting Lake Titicaca?

I could find no answers at the lake itself. But I did find a clue that pointed me onward. It came when I searched my memories of my first knowledge of the lake.

Cousteau's team had photographed a remarkable archaeological find in the waters of the lake itself: a man-made wall of massive blocks, fitted together by some process still unexplainable today.

The underwater wall stood at right angles to the shore. I checked a map. Following the line of the wall, straight as a crossbow shot, southeast across the silent flat tableland, a jeep would reach a well-known archaeological site in ten miles.

That site is called Tiahuanaco. I headed for it.

# IV

## Space Base One?

It was like a dream. I was racing far, far back in time, pursuing man's past across an empty land of mystery. The solitude swallowed me up.

Roads vanished into wilderness tracks of whitened rocks—faint traces of Inca highways—built during the Dark Ages of our own culture. Few Incas had stayed here long. Now the land seemed lifeless.

It wasn't quite lifeless, though. In the extraordinary clarity of the rarefied air, my senses were heightened. My eyes caught a few spots of sharp color moving in the farthest distance: brilliant pink, deep orange, and red. They were Indian women's skirts.

My mind worked on the thought of those Bolivian Indians. A strange people that lived on, seemingly bewildered, after their ancient world was dead. Why did they still wander this wide plateau in the sky? Since time immemorial it had been one of the poorest regions in the world. Its gritty soil could never have yielded enough for even the scattered little tribes to live decently.

Sheer inertia had held the Indians captive here, I supposed. Inertia and addiction to coca. Cocaine is derived from coca leaves. I had heard that the natives of the Altiplano chewed the leaves not to bring dreams and blow their minds, but to kill hunger pangs and give them an illusion of strength while working their meager fields. They believed it was di-

vinely given to them through their ancestors the Incas.

The thought of those half-starved people came
back to perplex me when I finished my beeline journey and found what was at the end of it. Could these
Indians' most distant forefathers conceivably have
created what I saw before my eyes? Could any small
group of people have built Tiahuanaco?

Tiahuanaco (pronounced Teah-wanako) is ruined
now, of course, but still awesome. Archaeological authorities agree that it is one of Latin America's major
architectural discoveries. They say it must have been
the center of an empire at some dim time before the
Incas. They seldom try to explain how it was built.
Erecting its massive stonework would require a hundred thousand people, unless they possessed colossal
power cranes or some secret of levitation unknown to
us.

This abandoned colony is strewn over the plain for
a sixth of a square mile. I wandered through it, trying
to imagine some explanation for it. Chilly winds
stalked the shadowed broken walls, picking up twist-
ing pillars of dust dancing high with them and let-
ting them dissolve, coloring the thin clear sunshine
with a threat of storm.

In that eerie light the ruins looked gaunt, melancholy, yet imposing. I moved along a courtyard, almost tiptoeing, for it was like entering a vast open library or museum in which the wind lived and the sun
glittered.

I passed the remains of great halls, platforms, enclosures, underground chambers. In the distance I
saw what might have been an artificial stone hill—or
was it a pyramid with a broad flat top? I peered into
the skeletons of empty granite houses. They were
priests' homes, some experts have written.

Gawking up at scattered monoliths as I advanced, I
tried to guess what they represented, but the
weathering of at least thirty centuries had left them
unrecognizable. Perhaps they were idols. Or decora-
tive statues. Or giant signposts. Their meaning had
gone down into darkness.

Except for one giant carving that looked somehow familiar. He wore a helmetlike cap, and a strange box on his chest. He might almost be a man in a space suit.

I kept coming back to thoughts of the people who lived here and disappeared as mysteriously as they came. I wondered what kind of beings they were, and what prophets they revered, and how they had built this place to last the ages through.

I know little about engineering. Yet even the most ingenious modern engineers were as baffled as I when they sought to explain how the structures here were built.

The walls are put together from megaliths—titanic many-sided stones, accurately cut and ground to a smooth finish, then fitted so precisely that no mortar is needed to bind them. There are no chinks in the walls. I couldn't even pound a chisel between the rocks.

I measured a medium-sized block. It was twenty feet by ten by three. This figured out to around fifty tons—a hundred thousand pounds—for it was hard Andean granite like most of the blocks. How many men would be needed to move one into place?

Then I remembered Cousteau's films of the drowned wall in Lake Titicaca—the wall that had pointed me straight toward this place. That wall was the same rock, and the same kind of stonework, as the walls here.

Investigators have found that each block in these walls is notched, so that it interlocks tightly with the stone underneath it, as well as with its neighbors on each side. Now, if you are a modern technologist, you can easily build such a wall.

You just suspend one megalith above another. You ease it down and measure off the uneven joining points. Then you lift it again, and set it on its side while someone blasts out the interface notches. Lift it once more, and see if it slides precisely into place with a tolerance of a few millimeters. If not, keep trying until it's right.

But if you don't have power tools and hydraulic lifts, how could you do the job?

Judging by the evidence, somehow the people at Titicaca and Tiahuanaca manipulated the giant blocks without wheels to roll them, without elephants or teams of oxen to pull or push or lift. And they chiseled them with only rudimentary bronze implements.

How did they do it? And the only answer that worked was—with nothing we know of on Earth.

Even a hundred thousand ordinary humans could not set up this mighty geometry unless they toiled for centuries—and how could they be fed meanwhile, in this barren wasteland?

I found myself remembering the fabled Cyclops with one big circular eye in the middle of their foreheads. They worked the quarries of Thrace, according to legend. It must have taken behemoths like the Cyclops to lift and fit the blocks at Tiahuanaco.

The sun and my fancies were making me giddy. I turned and strode on again, along a hall that led me up a short stone staircase.

As I climbed, I noticed that carvings jutted out from the walls at intervals. The carvings were faces. I had seen many arrays of carved faces around the world, but somehow these seemed different than might be expected. I would come back for a closer look later. First I wanted to see a single archway that remained at what was once the back of a temple.

It was a great gateway. It was hewn out of a single colossal stone, which I measured as ten feet high, twelve feet wide. Someone, somehow, had chiseled this gate from a block of andesite, an extremely hard volcanic rock—and had decorated it with intricate bas-reliefs.

I recognized it as the so-called Gate of the Sun, which I had seen pictured and discussed in so many books. Its name had probably been given to it by the Incas, in honor of their sun god. But it dated back far earlier than the Incas, so its original name was unknown.

Its frieze depicted row upon row of manlike birds

with strange faces etched in their eyes. Above them was a squat, standing figure wearing an elaborate headdress. His large face was squarish, with staring eyes from which round teardrops were descending, halted forever in mid-course.

This would be the far-famed Weeping God. Why did he weep? It was a perennial mystery. So were the smaller carvings below him.

No single artifact (with the exception, maybe, of the great pyramid at Cheops) has been mentioned so often in archaeological writings. None has generated so many theories to dispel the mysteries that shroud it.

One savant, after years of studying Tiahuanaco, has devoted a 433-page book to interpreting the intricate frieze on the Gate of the Sun. He concludes that the carving is a calendar. But, as with many other archaeological theories, a prime ingredient of this one is imagination.

According to his calendar theory, the solar year must have been only 298 days long when the frieze was carved. There were such years, contends author Hans Bellamy, about 11,500 years ago, at a time when "our moon was not yet the companion of our earth."

A temporarily moonless earth is just part of a scenario spun by Bellamy and others who believe that a succession of wandering moons circled our planet in aeons past. Each in turn was gradually drawn closer as it circled, until it came hurtling down to impact in a tremendous cataclysm, jolting the globe and obliterating all traces of highly advanced societies millennia ago.

Recent geological findings have discredited some of these assertions. But I'm still fascinated by the notion that a cosmic catastrophe could have doomed whole continental civilizations. Keep it in mind. It's an idea that crops up in various explanations of our beginnings.

When I had peered and pondered long enough at the Gate of the Sun, I moved out onto the open plain toward red-brown slopes, which would give me a

panorama of the dead settlement. As I walked, I
remembered other writings about Tiahuanaco.

Many conjectures have been made about this place.
But they are only farfetched guesses. Disciples of cold
science, who insisted on solidly linked facts as bridges
into the past, stayed silent on the sidelines. Thus they
tacitly admitted their inability to account for Tiahuanaco.

At least they knew that these impressive ruins were
already old when the Incas arrived. And they knew
that other evidence, radiating out from the cold
plateau, pointed back to it as the center of a complex
civilization that dominated all Peru and Bolivia. The
unmistakable symbol of the Weeping God was found
on ancient pottery and cloth in the farthest corners of
the Andes.

But no written language had been part of this
strange culture. Practically nothing turned up to indicate who the nameless empire builders were, or why
and how they built this headquarters in an isolated
fastness too cold for most crops and too empty of
game to support a large-scale city even if the dwellers
were great hunters. Tiahuanaco presumably remained
a remote and mysterious holy place ruled by priests
who might also have been warriors and hunters.

At last when the passes filled with armed men, and
the Inca armies in their progress southward from
Cuzco arrived to find these fragments of great buildings, they must have been mystified. According to one
folktale, they found among the blocks a tribe of Colla
Indians (whose descendants still live nearby). But
the tribe had no culture like that of the enlightened
builders of the colony, nor any knowledge of those
mysterious predecessors.

Putting together scraps of fact, modern researchers
guessed that the forerunners of the debased Collas
were themselves Collas who rose to a superb state of
culture about A.D. 600—and, sometime in the ensuing
three centuries built Tiahuanaco. Then around A.D.
900 their culture collapsed for unknown reasons and
they sank into the state of degradation in which the
Incas found them around A.D. 1200.

It was further supposed that the ruins dated from
two distinct pre-Inca periods, called by researchers
Tiahuanaco I and II. The relics of the first were
crude by comparison with those of the second.

Ah, well. In archaeology, as in society, position is
everything. Finding this under or over that may upset
a whole theory or confirm it. But at Tiahuanaco
pieces have been snatched out, pawed over, thrown
out of all arrangement, left with no record of where
they were found. How can anybody explain pottery
shards painted with pictures of a creature that paleontologists identified as a toxodon, a nine-foot brows-
ing beast like a short-legged hairy rhino, supposedly
extinct a million years ago? Such pots were unearthed
at Tiahuanaco!

Other guesses at dates when Tiahuanaco flourished
have ranged from as late as A.D. 800 to as early as 10,-
000 B.C. At any rate, the Incas learned much about architecture from the ruins, and they later applied this
knowledge in designing their own grand structures at
Cuzco, Machu Picchu, and other strongholds in the
Andes. They built thousands of miles of paved roads,
mountain stairways, farming terraces. Somehow they
also became expert dentists who could carve false
teeth and fit them in place, a feat unknown in other
ancient civilizations.

But they lived in the aura of the past greatness of
the shadowy Old Empire, whose ruined capital was
always there to give silent testimony that the Incas
arrived late and were not the first-chosen race they
claimed to be. Nevertheless, their remarkable dynasty
did emerge to reunite Peru. They proved that the
Weeping God of the cold plateau had not done his
pioneer work in vain.

When the Spaniards reached this place and made
inquiry in 1549 about the people who had created the
empty city, the oldest Inca then living could not tell
the chroniclers a single fact. Nothing was known. The
place had been built long before the Incas came, but
they were unable to guess who had built it.

Visitors of our day could contemplate much more
of Tiahuanaco, were it not for the sad fact that for

centuries it was used as a quarry. The Incas probably
and the Spaniards certainly hauled off many smaller
pieces of its structures for their own buildings. Some
of these became part of Spanish edifices in La Paz.
The church of the nearby Indian village, and a considerable part of the village itself, were obviously
made of materials from the ruins. And still Tiahuanaco, despite all this vandalism, remained a place of
grandeur and melancholy mystery. Since its nameless
builders departed, nothing approaching their culture
and engineering attainments flowered again among
their descendants.

But was it ever really a city?

The question nagged as I climbed the slope to get
a good view. A vague impression had crossed my
mind, as I walked through, that the place had been
far from finished when its builders left. The impression strengthened as I looked down.

There are scattered L-shaped or H-shaped sets of
walls standing alone, without the barest trace of walls
that should have abutted them. Granting that much
had been removed, why should some walls vanish entirely and others not at all?

Could this have been merely the beginning of a settlement, suddenly abandoned like Roanoke in our
own New World?

I harked back to the fantastic surmise I had made
at Lake Titicaca: ancient spacemen dropping from
the sky.

Let's consider Tiahuanaco as a possible continua-
tion of that surmise. Suppose it became a base for
those who might have colonized Earth. It could well
have been their first space base—and perhaps their
last.

Remember that the great lake's shoreline, at one
time, might have extended close to Tiahuanaco.
Water is essential to life as we know it, of course.
Water is also convenient for spacecraft falling from
great altitudes. So if Tiahuanaco were really near the
shore of the mountain sea, the idea that astronauts
built it becomes more plausible.

Locating a space base on a high, remote flatland

like the Altiplano might be logical for other reasons too. If we needed a site that could easily be defended against unknown marauders, there are few places on the globe as well situated. The plain was obviously uninhabited. Anyone approaching could be seen many miles away.

Given these facts, doesn't Tiahuanaco seem the likeliest place for starting a probe of Earth's environment?

Its elevation would make it as free of germs and gases as any area except the Himalayas, where few flats are to be found. Its flatness would make the first exploratory sallies a comparatively simple matter, just as our own first moon excursions were.

Remember what the Apollo crew did on the moon? First they established a safe base, and cautiously tested survival possibilities. Next they scouted the terrain close by, gradually widening their sweeps. They studied possibilities of creating shelter from materials at hand. They looked around to see if the supplies they brought with them could be augmented from any local sources. They made geological surveys. They pinpointed landmarks as navigation aids for longer journeys later.

And, of course, they reported results. Then they departed. But they kept always in mind the long-range objective of establishing a permanent base some day.

Let's say something like this happened about 10,000 B.C. or earlier. If the adventurers radioed back a report, it may still be spinning itself out toward other solar systems. Or maybe it was received by companion spacecraft circling somewhere nearby. Meanwhile the first arrivals—or a follow-on expedition, perhaps—could have dug in near their landing site.

The goal of explorers is to investigate and report. The goal of colonizers is to spread out and maintain themselves. Whichever they were, our imaginary crew from space had a good starting point.

If they could voyage across interstellar space, they were a far more advanced civilization than ours. Certainly their technology would be equal to the formidable task of quarrying rock, transporting it, and notching it to create solid interlocking walls.

Let's try to think ourselves into their place. What would we construct first? Probably a protective perimeter around our landing craft, I should think.

At Tiahuanaco there is an artificial ridge, outlining an enclosure approximately four thousand square yards in area. It has not been excavated.

I hear that the Bolivian government plans to dig there. It may find nothing, although there are said to be Incan legends of a honeycomb of tunnels at Tiahuanaco, and of great vertical shafts—somewhat like modern launch silos, I wonder? Or like the deep-hidden nerve center of our Strategic Air Command?

Any subterranean chambers at Tiahuanaco may have long since collapsed, or filled with dirt. Still, the solid evidence of that four-thousand-yard earthworks seems meaningful. Oh, I know the scholars ascribe it to some vague ceremonial purpose. But they have no proof.

I haven't any proof either.

Yet I think of the legends in many times and climes about a lost center of knowledge and culture. Some called it Atlantis, and said it had sunk beneath a sea. Some called it El Dorado, and located it in the unexplored interior of South America. Some thought that in Tartary—or was it in Abyssinia?—there reigned a priest-king called Prester John among huge mountains and vast deserts.

Those tall tales were so common, so widespread, that I find it hard to dismiss them as total bunk. A number of superstitions that we used to laugh at were eventually found to contain a germ of truth.

Maybe there were several wondrous cities lost in the depths of time. If so, Tiahuanaco could have been as wondrous as any. While I looked down on it from my vantage point, the fragments of my puzzle now had a faint trace of shape. I needed more individual pieces.

And I found them.

# V

## Who Was Viracocha?

In histories of Spain's conquest of Peru, compiled
from the archives of the Royal Academy of History at
Madrid, you'll find mentioned an obscure name that
echoes back through preconquest America: Viracocha.

The first Spaniard who came ashore in Peru was
greeted by this name. "Viracocha!" The natives spoke
it with awe and wonder. From then on they mur-
mured it often in saluting the newcomers.

As Pizarro's men began to understand the Inca language, they inferred that Viracocha meant something
like "foam of the sea," because the Inca word *cocha*
meant "sea." Although it might be a poetic fancy to
hail a landing party as seafoam, still it didn't quite
explain why these friendly natives spoke the name so
reverently and so often.

Journeying inland, Pizarro kept hearing himself
welcomed humbly as Viracocha. When he reached
the court of the great Inca emperor Atahualpa, he
discovered that the most learned men there had said
that he, Pizarro, might be the supreme Inca deity
come down to earth—a god called Viracocha, who
carried the title "Ancient lord, instructor of the world,
creator."

This puzzled Pizarro more than ever. But, as we
know from history, he didn't hesitate to take brutal
advantage of his hosts' inexplicable faith in him.

Not until years later, during long talks with the natives, did Spanish missionaries begin to unravel the puzzle of Viracocha.

William Prescott's classic history, *The Conquest of Peru*, which pieced together the smallest details left by contemporaries of Pizarro, sums up the padres' gleanings about the Inca god:

> A legend speaks of certain white and bearded men who, advancing from the shores of Lake Titicaca, established ascendancy over the natives and imparted to them the blessings of civilization.
>
> This may remind us of the tradition existing among the Aztecs in respect to Quetzalcoatl, the good deity, who with similar aspect came up the great plateau from the east on a like benevolent mission to the natives. The analogy is the more remarkable as there is no trace of any communication with, or even knowledge of, each other to be found in the two nations. . . .
>
> The Peruvians, like so many other Indian races, acknowledged a Supreme Being, the creator of the universe, whom they adored under the different names of Pachacamac and Viracocha.
>
> No temple was raised to this invisible Being, save one only in the valley not far from the Spanish city of Lima. Even this temple had existed there before the country came under the sway of the Inca.

Apparently the Incas had learned about Viracocha from their own lesser gods. He seemed to be a holy man from the sea. (The sea? Did that mean immense Lake Titicaca, or the remote ocean, which was only a vague rumor among Andean peoples?)

Whichever it was, the legends agree that when the Incas discovered the awesome empty settlement ten miles from Lake Titicaca, they were sure it had been built by the bearded white messiah and his followers.

Some legends told how this supreme teacher Viracocha had passed out of sight "over the same sea" when his work of creation was completed. (Creation? Had he created something more than an array of stone structures?)

In one version the holy man preached a farewell

sermon to a worshiping throng, and spoke of things that would happen in time to come. False prophets might arise but the people should not heed. Someday he and his helpers would revisit his people. Finally he "spread his cloak on the sea," stood upon it with his followers, and departed over the water.

A strange story.

On that continent where beards and fair skins were unknown, could any natives have invented it? To the Incas it was as real and important as the Gospels were to the Spaniards. Else why would they cry "Viracocha" at their first sight of bearded white men?

Siegfried Huber pointed out in his book *In the Kingdom of the Incas*, that their greeting to the strangers would be "utterly inexplicable in the absence of some preexistent tradition—that is, unless white, bearded men had been known in olden times and their return in later ages expected."

When the Spaniards heard the same tale of an ancient man-god in South America that had already startled them in two other lands, they were doubly flabbergasted. They knew a great deal by this time about the Aztec legend of Quetzalcoatl, a merciful hero who had been the human leader of the vanished Toltec as well as an immortal deity. He too was thought to be fair and bearded, and to have taught his people many things—how to farm more productively, how to work metal, how to construct beautiful buildings. But for some reason he had to leave his peaceful Toltec kingdom. He took his laws, his writings, his songs, and went away down the same road he had come. On a seashore he began to weep, then disappeared across the sea on "a raft of serpent skins." All the legends of Quetzalcoatl agreed that he promised to come again.

The Spaniards had also heard that in the vast, mysterious, hot forests of the old Mayan empire farther south, there had been a vague equivalent of Quetzalcoatl and Viracocha: a gentle king-god named Kukulcán. Sixteenth-century Bishop Diego de Lando, chief chronicler of Maya traditions, wrote down that Kukulcán built a great city, Mayapàn, ruled it for a period, then went away. The carved monuments at Mayapàn show him with a beard. On his ear he wears a jaguar claw.

Nobody knows how many thousand years the beardless brown Mayans fought the jungle in what is now Guatemala. There is only the dead stone record of their defeat. The jungle waited till the race grew old, and then closed in, driving them through slow centuries northward. There were only vestiges left when the white explorers came.

But at that time, in the sixteenth century, the Aztecs and Incas were still highly cultivated nations. They laid their lives trustingly in the hands of unknown newcomers, because those newcomers were white skinned and bearded, just as the legend said their returning god would be. Cortes and Pizarro were beneficiaries of a tragic case of mistaken identity.

Lost in the mists of fable, can Viracocha and Quetzalcoatl and Kukulcán be the same man seen through the wavering memories of three different cultures and their predecessors?

Unless we insist that they never existed at all, that imaginative storytellers made them up by sheer coincidence, can we avoid the likelihood that the three myths had the same origin much earlier in prehistory?

Of course there is another valid possibility: that three different bearded white missionaries from the same advanced civilization were set down at three different times in the desert of Mexico, the jungle of Yucatán, and the mountain-rimmed Altiplano; that they each brought the people food, energy, security, and surplus manpower on a scale undreamed-of earlier, by teaching the same arts and technologies (which would later diverge somewhat in the hands of three different empires); and that unknown external considerations eventually made all three leave by their own volition, sorrowing, with a promise to return, which apparently has never yet been kept.

If we accept the possibility of missions from outer space, we can imagine all this happening.

Maybe similar missionaries came to other parts of

the world at intervals of several millennia. We know of the Hebrew and Christian religious stories, preceded by even earlier Egyptian lamentations over the departure of man-gods. Many other peoples from China to Greece looked back to golden ages when war and strife were unknown and when, as Lao-tzu put it, one village might look at the smoke rising from the chimneys of another nearby without envy or rivalry.

"There is now enough anthropological and archaeological evidence to show that there is at least a partial basis for these wistful memories," wrote Lewis Mumford, one of the most encyclopedic scholars of our generation. "A great leap forward came to a climax about five thousand years ago." And there were notable leaps too, by certain other civilizations, at various later times.

Because of the Dead Sea Scrolls and many other recent discoveries throughout the Near and Middle East, not even the most skeptical can any longer dismiss the Bible as a poetic recounting of old fantasies. Scholars now agree that the Old and New Testaments are for the most part accurate records of events that really happened between about 3000 B.C. and A.D. 100.

Perhaps the earlier Mayan, Aztec, and Incan stories will someday turn out to be similarly well-grounded.

At Sacsahuamán, another fortress city of the ancient Andes, one of the remaining walls contains a singular rock. Nature has apparently chiseled into its carved face the figure of a snake standing upright on its tail, its head clearly defined in profile. According to local legend, before a battle, warriors thrust their fists into the crevice formed by the head. It was said to give them strength, courage, and magical powers to overcome their enemies. I might have been inclined to dismiss the story until I was shown what happened when a compass was placed in the crevice. To my shock, the needle began spinning as if agitated by some unseen force.

Scientifically it is relatively easy to account for the behavior of the compass. The rock obviously contained unusual electromagnetic properties. How did the so-called primitive inhabitant know that fact? Had someone with exotic knowledge at one time used the rock for its special potential?

If holy men with strange powers came from a faraway planet, which of them was first to arrive, and where did he land? For the many technical reasons I pointed out in the previous chapter, the Altiplano seems the most logical place in all the world for the very first astronauts' base to be set up.

I like to think that Viracocha might have been a living being who alighted on Lake Titicaca in a spacecraft, and who supervised the phenomenal construction work at Tiahuanaco, getting it done in his own lifetime with some yet-unknown technology.

This theory fits all the legends that the Incas believed so strongly that they put themselves at Pizarro's mercy.

Why shouldn't the Incas believe? Though they presumably never saw their white man-god, they saw the complex works he left behind. His teachings enabled them to build magnificent cities, first at Cuzco and then elsewhere.

And they were strengthened in their belief when Pizarro arrived, because Viracocha had promised to come again. (Obviously Viracocha wasn't clairvoyant, in the sense of being able to scan the future, or he would have foreseen Pizarro's coming and warned the natives not to obey the first white men they saw.)

It was said of Viracocha that he came into a world that had neither implements nor comforts, and that he presided over a time of "life without death."

I wonder what prompted the mythmakers to emphasize the lack of working tools. They certainly had at least crude stone tools. Could the story mean that Viracocha and his companions came equipped with "implements" like none ever seen before? Surely so, if they were voyagers from the stars.

Why was their stay a time of "life without death"? Conventional researchers ignore this as mere embroidery by those who handed down the legend. A yearning toward immortality has been almost universal. It's the staple of most myths and religions around the world.

Nevertheless, in the case of the man-god at the lake, I think it supports our hypothesis of an expedition that had plunged through space for untold centuries. Anyone who had done that had presumably put himself into a deathlike state of suspended animation for as long as need be, and then returned to life. That's one way to describe "life without death."

Furthermore, any interstellar expedition would probably possess medical skills that could heal people, or even restore life to the moribund. Our own laboratories are beginning to investigate drugs and cryogenic processes that may put patients into deep hibernation for long periods; maybe a more advanced civilization than ours once performed such feats before the eyes of awestricken people at Tiahuanaco.

Still another capability, far more miraculous, was also attributed to Viracocha by the Incas. Consider this Inca prayer to him, as translated and recorded by Alonso de Molina, one of Pizarro's men:

O Creator!
Ever-present Viracocha!
Thou who gavest life and valor to men, saying,
"Let this be a man."
And to woman, saying,
"Let this be a woman."
Thou who madest them and gave them being!
Watch over them, that they may live in health and
    peace.
Grant them long life, O Creator!

And now consider this Inca fable, as written down by a Spanish priest at Cuzco's first mission hospital about 1570:

In Tiahuanaco the Creator began to raise up the people and nations that are in that region, making one of each nation in clay. Those that were to wear their hair, with hair, and those that were to be shorn, with hair cut. When the Creator had finished making the figures of clay, he gave life and soul to each one.

We can hardly take that literally. And yet—I remember something that makes me wonder a little.

Those carved faces jutting out from the two walls that lead toward Tiahuanaco's Gate of the Sun.

The first time I had passed them, glancing briefly at a few, there had been a vague impression in the back of my mind that they weren't quite what I expected. But the impression wasn't bothersome enough to stop me, because I hadn't consciously expected anything in particular.

By the time I went to look at them again, I had read the Inca prayer and fable I've just quoted to you. Also, I had read in *Latin-American Mythology*, Vol. 13, a similar account of something Viracocha supposedly did at Tiahuanaco: "In this place he sculptured and designed on a great piece of stone all the nations that he intended to create."

Remembering those words, my flesh crawled a little as I looked at the stone faces. Now I knew what had seemed odd before.

The faces weren't really Indian—nor were they all the same, as you'd expect of a line of ornamental carvings. In fact, no two were very similar.

Elsewhere in Tiahuanaco were other carved faces but they were stylized, like totems or symbols. These near the Gate of the Sun were lifelike.

There were high foreheads and low foreheads, broad ones and narrow. Popeyes, slit eyes, deep-set eyes, slant eyes. High cheekbones and low cheekbones. A flat nose, a hooked nose, a snub nose, a fleshy nose that might almost be Roman with its bulging bridge. Thin faces, round faces, long ones, and short ones. Pointy profiles, straight profiles, bulging profiles. None was smiling. There were no headdresses or decorations.

The weathering of millennia had worn down the mouths and jawlines. I couldn't be sure whether these faces were bearded or not. Even so, they might easily be representations of "all the nations that he intended to create."

Contained in this "great piece of stone"—seventy or eighty feet of wall—was almost a gallery of mankind. Was it a catalog of types that already existed around the world? If so, where did the sculptor in the Andes find his models?

Or was it really a presage of shapes that a Creator intended to bring to life?

I've seen a book entitled *Art of Ancient America* by Disselhof. It was written in 1960, but the author might have been pointing a derisive finger at me as I am now when he wrote the following:

> There are two diametrically opposed points of view with regard to Tiahuanaco.
>
> In one camp are the romantics and dreamers who have called it "the cradle of mankind" and maintain that the Garden of Eden must have been situated on the shores of Lake Titicaca. Some of them have claimed that this pagan place of worship is more than ten thousand years old.
>
> In the other camp are modern scholars who endorse Bennett's theory that Tiahuanaco was a place of pilgrimage. This second interpretation, incomparably closer to the truth than the first, explains why Tiahuanaco came to be situated in barren mountain country which could never have provided the means of sustenance for a dense population.

I may well be a romantic and dreamer, but I think there are some facts on my side. As for the "modern scholars," they're curiously silent about how Tiahuanaco got built. Granted that the wasteland all around it "could never have provided the means of sustenance for a dense population," how do the scholars think this region supported a population large enough to build the sacred settlement?

Romantic and preposterous as the idea may sound (until you try to think of alternative explanations, and find none that seems to hold water) I've become

steadily more inclined to suspect that a handful of
spacemen were in fact the makers of Tiahuanaco.

As for the idea that one of them could bring clay or
stone figures to life, I boggle. I can harbor the theory
of "directed panspermia" as a basis for the legend, but
a more literal interpretation of the tale would seem to
violate all known laws of biology.

The Weeping God is another puzzle. Put it together with the carved faces. Does the combination
mean that the messiah at Tiahuanaco knew of an approaching cataclysm or Armageddon?

Maybe this prompted him or his disciples to sculpt
into the wall a record of their accomplishments in
populating Earth with varied breeds of mankind. If
nobody survived, the codex might remain to tell future colonists that someone had preceded them.

If, on the other hand, the Earthlings left behind
should manage to keep their foothold, the carvings
would remind them of their heritage. The legends
handed down would indicate that some did survive.

Maybe there was no cataclysm. Maybe Viracocha
was required to leave in compliance with some in-
scrutable master plan of experimentation or coloniza-
tion that we can't fathom. Possibly the beings from
another planet deliberately sent a series of expeditions at intervals, with instructions to stay only a
given length of time.

All these questions were in my mind when I was at
Tiahuanaco. But I didn't stay long to speculate about
them, because I knew of startling indications that the
space base at Tiahuanaco might have extended its
work beyond the Altiplano. To see what could have
been the astronauts' next operation, I hurried down
to the Peruvian coast.

# VI

## The Colossal Charts

Aircraft have shown us the true face of our continents. In all past centuries of history, roads deceived us.

Roads avoid the great lava beds, the mountain interiors, the sands, the buttes. They cater to man's need to move from stream to stream. They link villages—for between villages goods are traded and marriages are made.

Even when a road ventures across a solitude, it makes a dozen detours to seek its pleasure at every tiny water hole. Thus led astray, having traveled on so much well-watered soil to so many populated places, we have from the beginnings of our civilization embellished the picture of our prison. We have thought of our planet as mostly fruitful and populous.

But in this century our field of vision has immensely widened. The airplane taught us to travel as the projectile flies. Delivered from need of roads and towns and oases, we set our course for distant destinations. And then only, from the heights of our straight trajectories, did we perceive the bigger picture of rock and sand in which humanity, like a few weeds in an enormous prison yard, here and there has risked its precarious existence from time to time.

We to whom humble journeyings were once permitted have now been granted seven-league boots. We stride across mountains and barrens—and glance down to see tracks of old civilizations that in forgotten eras, by some miracle, bloomed like gardens.

Of all our discoveries from above, nothing has been more startling, I think, than the gigantic puzzle spread across miles of Peru's desert belt: not another dead city but a much stranger work of thinking beings.

As distances go in South America, I didn't have far to fly from the sky-high airport at La Paz down to the Paracas Peninsula. The Andes slid away below the window and were gone. Then a baked desert floor unrolled beneath me.

This was what geographers called the Atacama-Peruvian Desert. It was almost the only true desert in all South America, and the smallest anywhere in the world: a mere 140,000 square miles, about the size of Japan. It was also the most arid of all the world's deserts, with less than half an inch of rain a year on the average, which meant that it thirsted years at a time without a drop.

I looked down and tried to picture this wasteland as it must have been in those remote days when the great reptiles ruled the earth and man was still a dream of the far future. Had this been sea bottom? Not insofar as geologists could discern. Nor had it been jungle, forest, or grassland.

It was made from the iron-hard volcanic rock of the Andes. Vast geomorphic processees flattened and toasted it. Scoured by glaciers of past Ice Ages, perhaps—smoothed by broad forgotten rivers or pulverized bit by bit through eternal winds—it became a firm crust of powdered igneous metals.

Though it ended abruptly at the seacoast, the air masses from the Pacific sucked up its moisture instead of dropping any, for the cold of the Peruvian Current robbed clouds of their rain before they reached this land. Sailors called this the Rainless Coast.

I wanted first of all to scrutinize the desert's mysterious Nazca region at ground level. So I landed at the little city of Pisco, where a river threads its way across the desert to the ocean, midway down the Peruvian coast. Then I jeeped south.

What I had heard was true. There was almost nothing mysterious to be seen from the ground.

Out at the ocean's edge, on the Paracas Peninsula, I came to a broad declivity tilting steeply down from the plain to the Bay of Pisco. As I studied it from the top I saw nothing but a smooth thousand-foot face of rust-red rock. From the bottom I made out what seemed to be a few gopher burrows meandering up the palisade. That was all.

There were no ridges from which to get a higher view. So in all the centuries past, no earthbound eye could have discerned the strange marking I knew was on the face of this cliff, any more than an ant at the top or bottom of a slate could see anything drawn on it.

There was another place I must examine too.

I headed inland across the great cinnamon plain that passed into an opal mystery of great distances overhung by haze. The boom of the breakers died away behind me, and the heat hit me like a furnace blast, burning my skin like a mustard plaster, parching my throat, and scorching the roof of my mouth.

As I sped south and east the desert was empty. Nothing moved in it.

And nothing grew. Peruvians had told me that it lacked soil enough to grow a single blade of grass, as if it were blighted by a curse. Yet there had been big adobe villages, I knew, before the Incas came down from the mountains and overran them.

At various prehistoric times the Nazca people, the Chimu people, and the Mochica people had all dwelt hereabouts, near the banks of small rivers that meandered from the mountains to the sea.

Their civilizations had produced fine weaving and beautiful ceramics—and had left behind urns with pictures of the Weeping God, and stonework of the jaguar god. They must have been well-cultured peoples, for they understood how to make patterned irrigation canals and big stone reservoirs. This particular area had been Nazca territory clear out to the Bay of Pisco, according to tradition.

When I had driven sixty miles, I stopped. My compass, maps, and odometer told me this was where the mystery lay.

I saw nothing but miles of glaring wasteland all around.

In the solemn hush of that vast place, I emerged from my jeep and strode slowly along, studying the scorched desert floor. Its heat stung through my boot soles.

Now and then I passed a long straight depression, a foot or two wide. These were what I had come to see.

The indentations weren't conspicuous. If I hadn't been looking for them, I might not have noticed them. They might have been faint old paths—except that few footpaths are laid out so precisely.

They were few and far between—perfectly straight, but leading in various directions, sometimes stopping short, sometimes stretching away into the heat shimmer.

They were shallow—no deeper than a hand's breadth. At bottom they were pebbly and whitish. Since no dust storms ever swept this arid wilderness—and in fact few whispers of breeze ever stirred —the grooves could have been cut centuries if not millennia ago, and never yet have been buried or blurred or eroded.

Indeed, I knew that freak torrential rains had drenched the desert in 1925 and 1970, obliterating almost the last traces of the ancient adobe villages. But these scratches seemed as raw as if almost new. This must be one of the few places on earth where neither man nor weather had altered a construct from prehistory.

For these were constructed, beyond a doubt.

They were ruler straight, as if surveyors with theodolites had directed the cutting. And at places they intersected, making various neat geometric angles. No earthquake, no drying and cracking process of nature, could possibly have opened such undeviating rectilinear channels. Some vanished race had taken a lot of time and trouble to etch them distinctly into the ground.

I got back in the jeep and trailed one "path" for five miles. It never swerved even slightly. Climbing up and over a slope it stayed straight as a monorail track.

Finally it just ended. It pointed to nothing but the empty horizon.

Other lines did the same—or sometimes turned a precise corner and started in a new direction. If I followed them far enough, I came back to my starting point after several such turns; I had pursued a triangular or rectangular or polygonal course. But the area I circumscribed contained only sizzling acres of empty ground.

I noticed that some of these shallow troughs were broader than others. The broadest were five feet wide, the narrowest only a foot. The widths didn't seem to correlate with direction or location.

Later, roaming over the plain, I found an occasional trough that wasn't straight. Sometimes it swung around in a smooth arc. Sometimes it curled inside itself and ended, like the tail of a coiled snake.

But I didn't find one trough that gave me any clue to its purpose.

There never had been any settlements, shrines, or burial grounds marked off by these lines, as far as archaeologists could determine from minute inspection and judicious probing. In this featureless landscape the indentations had absolutely no visible meaning.

The Inca army had either failed to notice them or contemptuously ignored them; the empire's methodical engineers ran a twenty-four-foot-wide highway to the sea directly across groove after groove. In Spanish centuries the few wanderers across the hot desolation had not thought them worth investigating.

I might have thought likewise—had I not read about the eventual sensation caused by the lines I was looking at.

Having now satisfied myself that all these peculiar paths were barely discernible and utterly incomprehensible from the ground, I returned to Pisco. Next day I flew over the same areas I had traversed on the ground. How different they looked!

First I went out over the ocean, looked down at the thousand-foot slope by the Bay of Pisco—and saw an

apparition. A pictograph at least three hundred feet
high struck my eyes. It was carved so sharply, and
was so big, that it would be prominently visible from
many thousands of feet in the air. As soon as aircraft
had begun to pass this bay, back in the 1920s, the
sight had been reported and had become a major
puzzle to archaeologists.

While the picture was distinct, I wasn't sure what it
represented. It could be a trident such as Neptune
was imagined to carry. It could be an elegantly stylized tree. It could be a sort of pitchfork, or a sort of
candelabra—perhaps a variation of the Hebrew
menorah.

As I had verified the day before, only high-soaring
creatures could see the gigantic drawing. Until our
Air Age (and, perhaps, since some unknown earlier
Air Age) it had been invisible to mankind.

According to investigators who studied it and
turned away in bafflement, it predated the Inca
period. This meant that at least five centuries ago,
and perhaps much earlier, some old ones had drawn a
picture on a huge slate—for whom?

For someone in the sky, obviously.

But why? And how?

At least I could speculate on the how. Artisans had
probably cut it, guided by tracings laid down somehow on the rock face, or else by sophisticated engineers working from a precise diagram. The artisans
must have had some way of measuring the lengths
and directions of the lines they were carving, inasmuch as nobody on the ground could see them well
enough to direct them.

If there had been a tracing on the cliffside, some
hovering artist had sprayed it on, from a sufficiently
remote point to give him perspective—say a hundred
yards away, over the ocean. Incredible? Of course.

On the other hand, if there had been someone on
the ground directing the carving—as was done in our
own time with the faces carved on Mount Rushmore—he must have had an extraordinary system for
planning and measuring. Unlike the Rushmore operation, and unlike all mural paintings of which I knew,

this giant work was invisible to the supervisor as well as his workmen. Credible? Well, barely.

Whether it was made from tracing or from a master diagram, I felt sure the work implied a civilization far more advanced than historians had theorized. Such a civilization, for example, as the lost nation with its seat at Tiahuanaco.

No other artifacts, no stoneworks or skeletons had ever been found at the Bay of Pisco. Therefore the picture of the trident or candelabra or whatever it was must presumably have been put there by a distant, temporary outpost of whatever civilization drew it.

Assume that the Tiahuanaco civilization we have described did flourish, and did have some means of moving through the air. From Pisco to the Altiplano isn't far by air. If you needed a "blackboard" on which to draw a symbol that could be seen from over the ocean, and you wanted to place it so that it could be seen by travelers approaching from the north, your only choice would be this bay.

To my mind, the carving was a signal marker. Voyagers nearing the coast from the air could have used it as a navigational aid, or as a sign pointing the way to our hypothetical space city at Tiahuanaco. That site is approximately southeast of Pisco, and the trident points southeast.

Another possibility: it might have told the airmen that they were nearing the strange system of shallow troughs that lay sixty miles inland, also southeast. In their code, the tridentlike symbol might have denoted a particular distance.

I headed southeast, to see what these unknown fliers would have seen if the symbol had indeed led them across the desert en route to a rendezvous at Tiahuanaco.

When I neared the region I had reconnoitered by jeep the day before, I glanced down in that direction—and was startled again, even though I'd expected to see something remarkable.

In the middle of that immense staring burn upon the land, I thought I saw the runways of an airport.

There were two overlapping lines, wide enough to accommodate ten cars abreast, and roughly four thousand feet long. At ground level in the jeep I hadn't detected them at all. But in the air they were clearly visible from miles away.

Still, as I flew nearer I felt more certain that those strips had never been landing strips. Neither on the ground nor from the air was there any other clue to an ancient airport—no evidence of roads to or from the place, no grooves such as would have been worn into the soil by the weight of alighting vehicles, no indication that water had ever been stored there so that travelers and ground crews could refresh themselves.

But for many miles around, starting a few miles past whatever the quasi-airport was, I could see strange diagrams on the ground.

Those troughs or "paths" I had followed yesterday were the lines of the diagrams. There were patterns of straight lines, some meeting to form triangles and other geometrical shapes, some crossing or radiating in what seemed random polygons before they ended abruptly. But they were so neat that I felt sure they had been expertly surveyed.

More intriguing yet, the curved lines I'd seen were now understandable—in fact, unmistakable—as enormous drawings: of a bird, a spider, a fish, a jaguar, a whale, a man-shaped creature, and other designs of things unknown. The figures were 150 yards or more in width and length. They were ranged across that flat surface for many more miles than I'd explored yesterday. Without aerial photography or aerial supervision, nobody could have made drawings on such a scale.

I thought about it awhile. There below me on a tremendous drawing board was a message to the skies, a fairly complicated message. A human or superhuman consciousness had inscribed it. This was one of the very few places on the planet where it could have been permanently inscribed.

The code, the meaning, was lost, so that our race has never deciphered the message. Yet it struck me like a blow. In this vastness a sudden flash of intelligence had leaped across the centuries. Something had made known to us its existence.

Imagine yourself in a great building. It is empty as far as you can tell. Its doors are locked. Sitting alone in its silent center, you suddenly feel a breath on your cheek. What a presence! That was how I was affected by the desert charts and drawings.

Then another thought occurred to me. Those arrow-straight lines might not be totally indecipherable after all.

Look at a section of an airline map. The route lines crisscross in a random pattern, rather like the random lines I saw below. A pilot, having once established a base point on his map, read the lines as routes to be followed.

The Nazca lines might give a prehistoric aeronaut both routes and distances. In order to show distances, they would necessarily be different lengths. Thus the length of the Nazca lines could indicate distance, and their radiation would be directions.

Directions to what? To places on the globe where those unknown visitors had bases?

Maybe someday, I thought, a dedicated scholar would check through the mysterious maps that have come to us from antiquity and find an overlay pattern that would explain the Nazca lines. Meanwhile there was certain other information available.

For one thing, I knew approximately how old the desert drawings were. At the end of one line an archaeologist had once dug up a wooden "sighting" stump, and carbon-14 tests dated it at approximately A.D. 500—a thousand years before the Inca empire.

Furthermore, in 1941 Dr. Paul Kosok of Long Island University made a discovery about another line by playing a hunch. He thought the lines might have astronomical significance. So on June 22, the day of the winter solstice in the southern hemisphere, he stood in the desert and sighted along a line at sunset. The line pointed exactly to the sun as it touched the horizon. He was standing on a solstice line!

Later he checked other lines and got readings understandable to an astronomer. They concerned paths of planets, the sun, the moon, and various stars. Working from the hypothesis that the chart had been laid out early in the sixth century, he found that a chart of the heavens as it then existed would have corresponded with many of the lines. He decided that the geometric figures in the desert might well be "the world's largest astronomy book."

Nobody on the ground could have used the book. It would only be readable by, and useful to, aeronauts— or astronauts more likely, it seemed to me, because they would probably be unfamiliar with constellations as seen from Earth. They might need a star chart more urgently than aviators would.*

At any rate, pursuing the supposition I had formed in the Altiplano, if an expedition from outer space had actually splashed down at Lake Titicaca and set up its base at Tiahuanaco, one of its subsequent acts might well have been to lay out the giant navigational codex in the Nazca area to guide crews that came later.

What would the pioneer expedition do next? Or subsequently?

Suppose that laying out the codex took months or years of work, as well it might. Wouldn't this mean that quite a number of people would need to settle down awhile in the Nazca area?

Just as our own nation had established a complete new town in the middle of nowhere at Oak Ridge, Tennessee, for the Manhattan Project—the development of the first atomic weapons—maybe an earlier and more peaceful civilization had put a colony in the Atacama-Peruvian Desert for the big project of the giant codex.

I wondered what sort of people had lived in that area in prehistoric times. To find out, I delved into reference books.

"Flourishing independently but contemporaneously with classic Tiahuanaco, Nazca was apparently under

---

* When the astronauts of Skylab II checked Nazca (inspired in part by the television special "In Search of Ancient Astronauts," they reported that they could see lines but there was no special meaning or message they could read.

Tiahuanaco influence until the Inca conquered the region in the fifteenth century. Little is known of the people. No villages or buildings can be positively identified as Nazcan. Examples of the skilled ceramic and textile arts are, however, found in burial pits. Highly polished, expertly designed and with polychrome paintings, the pottery is unlike that of other Peruvian cultures." (*The Art of Ancient Peru*, Ferdinand Anton)

Approximately 225,000 pots of Nazcaware had been found—enough for quite a sizable colony. The pottery was mostly broken into shards, as ancient containers usually are when uncovered by modern diggers. Earthquakes or the weight of earth slowly piling over them, simple domestic accidents while the pots were in use, these were among the causes that so often broke up anything breakable before the excavators and reconstructors arrived. Beside, pottery buried at grave sites was "killed" or broken so it could join its master wherever death took him.

When archaeologists painstakingly fitted together the shards of the shattered Nazca pots, certain surprising patterns emerged.

Any typical pot bore a set of painted or glazed faces, and each face on a given pot was strikingly different. The skins of the faces were of different shades ranging from white through yellow and brown and copper to black, as if they represented the various races that dwelt on Earth. And the faces had such dissimilar physiognomies that I was strongly reminded of the faces on the wall at Tiahuanaco.

But beyond this, there was an even more remarkable decoration on many of the pots: clear pictures of llamas. What was remarkable about the llama pictures was that instead of having only two toes, or the cloven hoof, as llamas do now, those on the pots had five toes on each foot.

Paleontologists say that llamas did have five toes thousands of years ago—at a time when men supposedly were still in the Stone Age, just beginning to use tools, and much too primitive to make pottery.

Very well. I was satisfied that the old ones who

built such an advanced complex of buildings at Tiahuanaco could very well have put down roots in the Peruvian desert too. Presumably the people who did the work of making the gigantic charts and drawings had stayed on in the area, living out their lives and establishing permanent homes, which were used by generation after generation for almost a thousand years, until the Incas came and systematically wiped out all records and memories of earlier people.

Meanwhile, still following my hunch that something previously unknown on Earth had been hereabouts, I asked myself what else might have happened after the sky messages had been put in place. What would the visitors do beyond this?

Further expansion, perhaps? Missions to a few other parts of South America, or to more remote lands?

If so, then the colonizers might have wanted to put other "road maps" or signposts or messages near these other places to guide incoming aeronauts or astronauts. Was there any evidence that this had been done?

Much of the evidence, if it ever existed, would necessarily have been obliterated later on. Erosion, floods, earthquakes, new settlers on the land—many things would be likely to wipe out, or cover over, ancient oversized drawings or charts almost anywhere in the known world.

Nevertheless, explorers had found a few sets of markings that might have served the same purposes as those in Peru.

One set was found in another desert—the Mojave Desert of California. About a hundred miles up the Colorado River, almost hidden to ground-level eyes, and almost inaccessible among towering rock buttes, there is an array of neatly cut trenches in dry lake bottoms. It is called the Mojave Maze. The Mojave Indians who now live thereabouts have always insisted that their own ancestors didn't construct the maze; it was there before their tribe came, they say.

Prehistoric people likewise cut strange petroglyphs onto the walls of Titus Canyon in a remote part of

Death Valley. There are depictions of sheep and liz-
ards. There is something like an upside-down candelabra. There are various triangles, diamonds, zigzag
lines, and one incomplete set of wavy lines radiating
from a central circle—as if to indicate, perhaps, that
someone had gone out in six directions from one central location but had not gone out in other directions.
Authorities argue about the meanings, but the old
runes have kept their secrets.

I also heard of fainter, scantier straight "roads" that
led nowhere but formed peculiar patterns in the remote Zana and Lambayeque valleys of northern
Chile. Perhaps the old ones expanded mostly in Latin
America, with just a few other air bases in the flat-
lands of such places as the ancient California deserts.
Or conceivably they had many bases, and the air
markers pointing to them were erased by time.

I did discover one interesting scrap of evidence
that seemed to indicate that somebody at Nazca was
familiar with the depths of the Amazon jungle.
Among the giant drawings in the Nazca area was one
depicting a spider. It was quite a clear, precise
drawing of a spider with a definite distortion at the
end of the third leg. Entomologists, studying air photos of the drawing, said that it depicted a variety of
spider called the Ricinulei, which is unique among all
spiders. The Ricinulei spider exists only in the
Amazon jungle.

Having ascertained all I could about huge prehistoric pictographs and charts, I looked around to see
where my theory might lead me next. Where could
the hypothetical civilization from space have left any
other kinds of clue?

Much terrain that is now underwater might have
been dry land when the old ones were on the planet.
So I canvassed for connecting links on shallow ocean
bottoms. And I found one.

# VII

## Something to Make the Gods Weep

The water was warm and clear. The diving was easy. I was a little more than a thousand yards offshore at Bimini and looking out of the face mask I saw a rock formation that made my skin prickle. The walls of Ollantaytambo and Tiahuanaco were duplicated on the ocean floor. Years of coral encrustation had given them a dead white cast, but the peculiar notched joining points were there. To me, the hand of the master builders of the Altiplano was clearly visible. So this was where they had come.

The first time I heard of the Bimini Wall was in a conversation with Alan Jay Lerner. The poet and lyricist, better known for *My Fair Lady* than his work in archaeology, had been on expeditions searching the Caribbean floor for evidence of extraterrestrial visits in the region. He was sure that the Bahamas held important clues. My sighting at Bimini confirmed his description.

I was a relative latecomer to the site. It had been subjected to intensive study by a number of experts. Some had declared that the formation was natural. The factor that belied their findings to me was positioning of the individual pieces of wall. I can understand underwater channels eroding channels in a rock face, but I had never encountered a current that could carve right angles and precise notches.

There are still other sites than Bimini in the Bahama Banks where "hard" evidence of earlier civilizations can be found. The problem of locating them was the jealousy with which they are guarded. The high price of antiquarian objets-d'art has made archaeological finds as valuable as the fabled Spanish treasure ships. Unscrupulous divers were all too ready to poach on any new discovery. It made research all the more difficult. As soon as I broached the subject to a professional, I was met with tight-lipped suspicion. When I finally succeeded in convincing individuals that I was on a legitimate quest for information, and not a threat to their find, they relaxed somewhat. Still anonymity was the rule. As one diver put it, "Look, you give out my name and a description of my find, and seventeen guys who know roughly where I've been diving will be down there scrounging up my hard work."

I promised anonymity and got more promising information.

"I dove and I found fourteen buildings," one underwater explorer told me. His voice cut through the drowsy surge of the surf and there was a little pause. I needed an instant to digest his rather startling news. He was telling me of a reconnaissance he made in the Bahama Islands. The Bahamas are seven-hundred-odd islands—the "golden archipelago," they have been called—scattered over ninety thousand square miles of ocean water just east of Florida and Cuba.

"Where did you dive?" I asked.

"Off Andros Island, you know?"

Few Americans do know much about the Bahamas outside Nassau. But because I was especially interested, I knew Andros.

It is a hundred miles long, the one big island in all the Bahamas. There are parts of its wooded, water-veined interior where man has never been. Only a few tiny villages dot its coastline. For all its size, and despite the fact that it is only fifteen minutes west of Nassau by air, Andros is one of the least-visited places in the Bahamas.

I said, "You probably didn't dive on the east side of it, did you?" East of the island the undersea canyon called the Tongue of the Ocean drops down a thousand fathoms deep. But on the other three sides are the Great Bahama Bank, which stays shallow halfway to Florida.

"Hell no!" he growled, but would go no further.

"OK. What sort of buildings did you find?"

"Stone buildings. Limestone. The walls are four feet thick."

"Well, that figures," I mused. "Limestone would be the logical building material anywhere in the Bahamas."

Limestone, of course, is a sedimentary rock, formed by the ocean's weight slowly crushing down the fossils of trillions of long-dead sea creatures. I knew there was limestone under the whole Bahama complex.

He said, "Oh, sure, limestone would be the rock you'd use around here, if you were going to construct stone buildings. If!"

"You mean the natives never did?"

He shook his head. "When Columbus got here, he didn't find a single stone building, nor the ruins of any. In fact no Indians in the whole Caribbean built out of stone. They lived in thatched huts and limestone caves."

"How about the Spaniards?"

"They were too busy digging gold out of South America ever to settle these islands. And anyhow, the walls I found down there are much better built than Spanish walls."

"Better built in what way?"

"They're made of big blocks of beautifully square-cut stone, tightly fitted together."

"Hmm. Square-cut blocks sound like all those construction jobs in the Andes," I said.

I glanced thoughtfully out to sea. The trade wind ruffled soft white plumes through a sparkling green surf. I kept thinking how far Tiahuanaco is from Andros Island! The trip would have required an airplane, unless they worked their way down through those towering mountains, walked up the Pacific Coast and across Central America, then voyaged clear up through the Caribbean past Haiti and Cuba and most of the Bahamas.

"Are the buildings close together?" I asked.

"Some are close, a couple of hundred yards apart. Some of them are five miles to the next one."

"Tell me about one of the biggest buildings, will you?"

"One was 240 feet long and 80 feet wide, and made into three different rooms. No windows. No floor that I could find—it might be deep under the sand."

"What do you think the building was?" I asked.

"Maybe a temple. I know this much, there's a temple in Yucatán that has the exact same floor plan. Some people call it the Temple of the Dwarfs, others the Temple of the Turtles. It's at Uxmal. I've been all through that temple, and it sure as hell has the same configuration."

I needled him a little. "Couldn't that structure be a fish trap, or a storage pen for turtles or sponges after they were caught?"

"Naw, I know that's what archaeologists said about those other shapes off Bimini. But this wasn't somebody building a turtle pit under water. Why would anybody engineer a turtle pit into such an exact rectangle? Why cut up such thick blocks of limestone and drag them out from shore? Why fit them together so perfectly? This was no more primitive than the walls in Peru."

We talked for a long time. He told me how he had dug several holes next to the biggest building, down there in the green silence. He found buried pottery and ceramic figurines. But he could not even guess what civilization had made them.

And so his investigation hit a dead end. For two years he sent photographs to experts all over the world, never finding one who had seen similar pots and figurines. Nobody would risk classifying them, even as to possible area of origin, for fear of ridicule from some other expert.

"They're all afraid to get involved in this whole Atlantis controversy," he told me later.

However, he did get one interesting clue. There are scientific tests that can be made on anything that has been fired in a kiln—tests by which its age can be roughly estimated. The tests seemed to suggest that these articles had been made between 5000 and 3000 B.C. There the puzzle rests today.

Underwater archaeology is one of the newer branches of science. It only became practical in 1942 when Jacques Cousteau invented his aqualung or scuba (self-contained underwater breathing apparatus). This wondrous gadget enabled skilled divers to prowl the bottom of the sea thus opening up nearly two million square miles of drowned land to detailed investigation.

In French and British undersea caves, divers found rich pre-Christian relics and some of the world's oldest murals. In the Mediterranean they found assorted clues to the great ancestors of western civilization, who all had sailed those seas: Egyptians, Phoenicians, Etruscans, Greeks, Romans. In the Bahamas, I thought, they might find the most interesting clues of all.

"There's a lot of water in the Bahamas," sailors have said, "and much of it's spread thin." The seawater on the shallow shelves is the world's clearest because there are no rivers on the islands (except for little Goose River on Andros). Aircraft have often reported sightings of walls, buildings, plazas, and causeways a few fathoms down in those crystal plains. There are even rumors of a four-acre citadel off Cuba.

But I couldn't sift fact from fiction in such reports. Finds are often lost again soon after they're seen, as the shifting sands on the bottom cover them. Nevertheless my prowlings in the Bahamas established certain facts to my own satisfaction.

The whole Bahama Banks area is a land mass that was above sea level until fairly recently, as geologists and archaeologists reckon time. Why am I sure of this? Look at a depth map of the ocean around the Bahamas. Take a pencil and fill in the sea area less than fifty feet deep. You'll see an enormous island, indented by sections of the true ocean including the underwater canyon, Tongue of the Ocean, which thrusts deep into the Bahama Banks directly east of Andros.

Divers have felt their way down the clifflike eastern

base of Andros. In the face of that declivity they have
found underwater caverns and grottoes, studded with
stalactites and stalagmites. Stalactites are formed
from the slow trickle and evaporation of mineral-bear-
ing water; obviously there couldn't be evaporation under the sea. Stalagmites rise from a cave floor as
water drips from its ceiling and deposits grains of
minerals; water couldn't drip unless it had air space
to drip through. So the caves had to be on dry land
during the long ages when those rock formations were
being created.

Why did I say the Bahama Banks were "recently"
dry? Geologists are certain that in the last Ice Age
there were vast masses of ice reaching all the way
down to Wisconsin—and that the ice sheet started its
slow retreat northward about 9000 B.C. In the following centuries, as mountains of frozen water melted
inch by inch and then foot by foot, the ocean rose,
probably four hundred feet or more above its previous level during the millennia when so much water
had been trapped in glaciers. The rise inundated ancient islands and the coastal shelves of continents.

It was in that "recent" period—say between 8000
and 2000 B.C., at a loose estimate—that dwellers on
what are now broad underwater plateaus must have
had to abandon their settlements. The preflood peoples who survived would surely have handed down
unforgettable legends of the rains, floods, and en-
croaching seas that overwhelmed them.

To me this was the explanation of the Old Testament story of the flood, and of strikingly similar stories among native tribes and cultured civilizations in
many parts of the world.

Among the ruins of Ur in Mesopotamia, I knew,
were countless evidences of a catastrophic flood that
deposited a layer of clay nine feet thick; clay tablets
from Nineveh described an epic battle against a moving layer of mud that leveled the ground until it was
"flat as a roof"; flood legends persisted for centuries in
Australia, India, Polynesia, Tibet, Kashmir, even
Lithuania.

The same geological and archaeological findings

were the explanation, it seemed to me, of the sunken ruins in the Mediterranean and Aegean seas, of the stone buildings a few fathoms deep in the Bahamas— and of the references in old Greek and Latin writings to lost continents, mysterious islands, and forgotten cities which "disappeared into the sea."

Oh, I could agree that a few of these places probably sank suddenly because of earthquakes. But the likeliest explanation for most of them was simply that they were engulfed in times of catastrophic floods after the last Ice Age.

Such catastrophes would certainly be cause for weeping by any colonizers from outer space who had preached and taught and built new missions here and there, only to find that the sea's inexorable rise was putting their colonies under water.

If they suspected that the water might continue rising until it covered all but the high mountains, supermen like Viracocha and/or Quetzalcoatl and/or Kukulcán might well have soared away in a spacecraft, vowing sadly to return at some unforeseeable future time.

Let's suppose that Tiahuanaco was the first base of beings from another world. Let's suppose further, as we've already done in previous chapters, that these beings sent emissaries down through the Andes, mixing their sperm with that of the natives, and put great silent signals in the Peruvian desert to guide spacecraft arriving later. What might have been their next step?

My surmise was that the next step was to build another base in what was then a broad, pleasant land: the Bahama plateau.

Admittedly the only solid evidence, so far, to support this conjecture was the style of architecture of those limestone walls. The big, precisely cut and fitted blocks were more similar to the Andean ruins than to any other buildings yet found on earth. But even if the building style should eventually turn out to be somewhat different on closer inspection, I would still ask, Where did the unknown builders at Andros get the technology to cut and manipulate such big cubes of stone?

Archaeologists had found no signs of good engineering or high technology used by prehistoric people elsewhere in the Bahamas—or anywhere in the West Indies, in Cuba or Haiti or any other Caribbean lands, or even on the Atlantic seaboard of the Americas.

What tools were used to cut those building blocks at Tiahuanaco, at the Inca cities, and by implication at Andros?

They must have been highly efficient yet fairly simple and compact tools, because the users apparently were able to bring them from great distances.

Almost certainly, then, they were power tools of some kind. Yet I saw nothing in the Bahamas that would suggest a prehistoric power source. Mineral materials were scarce. Waterpower was hardly a possibility. The source must have been something more exotic, something still unknown to modern science.

I found one vague clue to that power source. The clue lay in another abiding mystery that had hung over the nearby ocean region for many years.

# VIII

## *Voyages Into Limbo*

On December 5, 1945, a group of five U.S. Navy bombers designated as Flight 19 took off from Fort Lauderdale, Florida, on a routine training mission. Flying formation, they disappeared southeastward over the shimmering horizon toward where the Bahamas lay. It was two o'clock on a warm clear afternoon.

An hour and a half later Flight 19 was noted to be overdue to return. The Naval Air Station began trying to reach it by radio.

There was no response for a while. Then the voice of the young lieutenant in charge of the flight, Charles Taylor, came over the air:

"Calling tower—this is an emergency. We seem to be off course. We cannot see land. Repeat, we cannot see land."

The controller in the tower demanded, "What is your position, Flight 19?"

"We're not sure—we seem to be lost."

Mentally cursing the stupidity of young pilots and navigators, the controller growled, "Fly due west. In a few minutes you'll sight the mainland."

"We don't know which way is west," Taylor answered. "Everything is strange—even the ocean." He was obviously agitated.

There was more static than usual. The Naval Air Station could make no sense of brief garbled messages that followed. It was sufficiently perplexed and uneasy to put emergency procedures into operation.

Thirteen seasoned airmen scrambled into a big Martin Mariner for a standard search-and-rescue mission under Lieutenant Robert F. Cox, the senior flight instructor at Fort Lauderdale. As soon as this rescue plane had gained altitude over the ocean, Cox radioed: "Flight 19, I'll fly south to meet you and guide you back. What's your altitude?"

Taylor's reply was indistinct until his last four words, which were clear: "Don't come after me."

The incredulous listeners in the control tower thought they heard Taylor radio to Lieutenant Edward Powers, another of the Flight 19 pilots, to take command of the flight. A little later someone—presumably Powers—said, "We're not sure where we are. We're completely lost."

Nothing more was ever heard from Flight 19, although each of its five planes had a radio transmitter.

Meanwhile Cox, at the controls of the rescue craft, kept it climbing to get a broader view of the ocean and skies. His crewmen scanned with binoculars in all directions. For seven minutes he kept in touch with the control tower, reporting no downed planes or wreckage sighted in the probable crash zone.

Then he apparently stopped transmitting. Nothing more was ever heard from the Martin flying boat.

As the period of silence lengthened, more search planes went. They had no difficulty maintaining radio contact with the tower and with each other, but they saw nothing. The sky was clear and the ocean was calm.

Fishing boats and coastal steamers converged on the area. Air Force bases in Florida sent planes to help search. Since the Avenger bombers of Flight 19 could be expected to remain afloat for hours after even the most inept crash landings on the water, someone seemed certain to sight them soon. But no one did.

Nor did anyone see the Martin flying boat. Next morning a great air and sea search spread across the Atlantic as far eastward as Bermuda and Puerto Rico, north toward Canada, south through all the Bahamas and beyond.

Nothing was found.

The searchers could not believe it, nor could the stunned officers at Fort Lauderdale. It was incredible that six big aircraft could vanish silently at the same time, over the same sunlit stretch of ocean, without at least leaving visible clues on the water.

All six planes carried emergency rafts. Their twenty-seven men were equipped with life jackets. The Mariner rescue plane carried full equipment to operate in any weather, and an auxiliary radio as well as its regular set.

Eventually the navy presumed the men dead, and notified their families. After a terse announcement to the press, it hid under a blanket of official silence. Although a naval court of inquiry was convened, its proceedings remained secret. For twenty-nine years no information was forthcoming about the most bizarre mystery in the annals of aviation.

However, from 1945 to 1973 one man kept seeking more facts about it. He was Art Ford, a radio newsman now with *Penthouse* magazine. Finally he wrote a book called *The Bermuda Triangle, Best-Kept Secret of Our Time*, to be published soon. I asked him about his investigation.

"Year after year the parents of the boys who disappeared kept asking questions," he told me. "Why was there no wreckage? Why no bodies? But the navy wouldn't talk. It kept a seal on the minutes of its secret inquiry in Miami Beach."

"Would anyone outside the navy have any clues?" I asked. "Maybe some civilian radio operators happened to hear the air controller's talk with the planes."

"Yes, I thought of that. And eventually I found a few ham radio operators who actually did hear some of the transmissions. One man in Florida gave me his written record that the pilot in command, Lieutenant Taylor, said something over the air that sounded like 'They look like they're from outer space—don't come after me.'"

A little shiver went down my spine. I said, "But you had no way to confirm that, did you?"

"Not for many years. But finally, because of the new Freedom of Information Act, I got access to the transcript of the closed investigation. On page 72 of the official record I found testimony that the tower heard the senior flight instructor talking over the radio to Charles Taylor, who commanded the flight. What Taylor said was garbled. But here again, just as the ham radio operator heard, the navy man in the tower swore he understood a clear phrase at the end, 'Don't come after me.'"

"What do you think that meant?"

Art threw up his hands. "All I know is that Taylor saw something that caused a formation of five aircraft to leave this earth. He was evidently caught in some predicament he hadn't been trained for. This wasn't the rambling of some crackpot who thought he saw something in the back forty one night when he had too much cider. This was a clearcut observation from a man in charge of fourteen lives and five planes."

"Those radio messages sound as wild and sinister as if they came from a madhouse," I muttered.

"Yeah. Why should Taylor say he was lost? What did he mean when he said the ocean looked strange? Why would he say to a rescue mission, don't come and find my men and our planes?"

"He must have seen something out there over the ocean."

"Maybe he saw some kind of vehicles, objects, spacecraft—I don't know. Maybe there was something surrounding him, or coming into view, that was so powerful and so totally alien to our way of life that he felt he had to warn other planes."

"But what could have happened after that? What became of Flight 19 and the rescue mission?"

"They went somewhere, didn't they? If they didn't go down, did they go up? Were they carried away into outer space? I don't know. I have no theory. But the established facts are bound to make me wonder, have we ever been visited?"

"Well, that brings us," I said, "to the part of this

mystery that I'm especially curious about—the geographic aspect of it. If we were visited, do you see any reason why the visit should occur in this one small sector of ocean?"

"Oh, sure. The planes vanished in an area which is now our space-shot sector. The same reasons that make the East Florida coast ideal for rocket shots into space might also make it ideal for landings from outer space."

"Why is it an ideal area? What's different about it?"

"It's open ocean, so a crash over populated cities isn't a strong possibility. It's off the normal air lanes, so an air collision is very unlikely. Most important of all, that broad ocean corridor southeast from the Cape Kennedy-Fort Lauderdale starting point is bounded by islands that could be guideposts or emergency landing places. In other words it's never more than five hundred miles from a landing spot, or less than two hundred. And it's easily recognized from great altitudes."

I produced a map. Art ran his finger along the lane he was describing.

"Follow it farther," he said. "See? After brushing the northeast tip of South America it continues across thousands of miles of open ocean—clear to Africa. Outward bound or inward bound, a spacecraft has a long clear run with good guideposts. This channel is the perfect doorway to space. And the door opens both ways."

I said, "I keep thinking about that statement from one of the disappearing pilots—'Even the ocean looks different.' Maybe all six aircraft flew into some disturbance that disrupted their navigation equipment and eventually silenced their radios.

"Did you get any clues to any perceptible disturbance during that afternoon in 1945?"

He nodded. "I looked into it. And I found a couple of reports—not specifically for that day, but for a period of weeks or months in late 1945."

I waited expectantly.

He went on after digging through some notes. "Two widely separated observatories happened to detect peculiar phenomena in the sky. At the Mount Wilson observatory, Joel Stebbins found that the night sky was giving off intense infrared radiation. Nobody had ever noticed anything like that before, or has since, as far as I know.

"And over in the Netherlands," he went on, "at the Lieden observatory, there are records that the radio-wave portion of the spectrum brought in remarkably strong signals from parts of the sky. The Lieden people reported, and I'm quoting them, 'An entirely new window had been opened on the heavens.' It makes me wonder if visitors came through that window, and took our planes back with them."

Having learned all I could from Art Ford, I went off to search through old records concerning the section of ocean that he called the Bermuda Triangle.

I found that the six planes from Fort Lauderdale were part of a greater mystery. For at least two centuries, unexplained disappearances had kept occurring in that area.

Take a map and put your pencil on Bermuda. Draw a line from there west to Cape Canaveral on the Florida coast. From there, draw a short line southeast through the Bahamas—then northeast again to Bermuda. This is the Bermuda Triangle, about three-hundred thousand square miles of open sea. Neither ships nor aircraft cross it often. It does not lie between places where there is much travel or commerce.

But when someone does cross that lonely triangle, he had better beware. Within this comparatively small patch of ocean, more than a hundred ships and aircraft have been permanently listed as missing during the last two hundred years. Not one, so far as I could learn, sent any distress signal, or left any wreckage or lifeboats visible to searchers.

There was one exception of a sort. The London *Times* for November 6, 1840, reported that the *Rosalie*, a large French ship bound from Hamburg to Havana, was found drifting near the Bahamas. Most of its sails were set, but there was nobody aboard. Its valuable cargo was intact. The ship was not leaking, nor was there any other sign of trouble. A canary was twittering in a cage. Nothing was ever heard of the vanished officers and crew.

Here are other sample incidents from the list I compiled.

In January 1880 the British training ship *Atalanta* sailed from Bermuda with 250 cadets and sailors aboard. It was never heard of again.

On March 4, 1918, the *USS Cyclops*, a Navy fuel ship, left Barbados bound for Hampton Roads, Virginia. The ship was a big one, about a city block long. It carried ten thousand tons of manganese ore, and 309 passengers and crewmen. It reported no problems during its routine radio transmissions during the first half of its trip. Then there were no more messages. American destroyers combed the western Atlantic for her, but found nothing—not even the debris or oil slick that was characteristic of ships sunk by submarines. Nevertheless, World War I was in progress, and a U-boat sinking seemed the only tenable theory, even though German submarines were hardly likely to choose that part of the Atlantic for their operations. After the war, records of the German Admiralty showed that the *Cyclops* had not been attacked nor even seen by German submarines, which truly had never been anywhere near the Bermuda Triangle.

In January, 1962, a KB-50 air force tanker with a crew of eight flew into the Triangle and vanished.

In March, 1963, the *Sulphur Queen* was lost with thirty-nine aboard. In July of that same year a fishing boat called *Sho' Boy* disappeared with forty aboard. On August 28 two giant Air Force tankers, each powered by four jet engines, flew together into the area, and passed into limbo.

In 1970 a cabin cruiser and a small plane disappeared in the same area in a single month.

The disturbance, if such it is, in the Bermuda Triangle may have started much earlier than we know. Shakespeare made a cryptic reference to "the still vex'd Bermoothes" in *The Tempest*. Then, as now, the Bermoothes meant the small archipelago in the Atlan-

tic, known today collectively as Bermuda, lying about
650 miles southeast of Cape Hatteras.

Shakespeare might have meant the frequency of
shipwrecks near the little islands, whose coral reefs
are dangerous. Divers have found the graves of some
120 ships near that sunny archipelago. But "vex'd"
seems an odd adjective for reefs.

At least we know what happened to the ships that
disappeared near Bermuda in Shakespeare's time. As
for all those other missing vessels and people of
whom no trace was ever found, could they have been
seized and spirited away—"taken up," as Art Ford
phrased it—by some agency unknown to the inhabitants of this earth?

Or could something have suddenly and silently va-
porized them?

Or did something sink them, or suck them down, so
quickly that nothing was left behind for searchers to
see?

I don't know, of course. But I think there is a
likelier possibility, somewhat more complicated.

Assume that there was a space colony on the
Bahama plateau, as that area would have been before
the oceans rose. Assume further that the colony had
an exotic technology to utilize. What if the men from
space eventually jettisoned their power source, or ac-
cidentally dropped it, in deep water somewhere
within the Bermuda Triangle?

Conceivably that unknown source of energy might
still emit radiation of some kind from time to time,
triggered by random natural causes or by the passage
of a ship or aircraft across invisible beams. I can
imagine this ruining electronic equipment, disorganiz-
ing human nervous systems, perhaps subsequently
wreaking such total destruction that nothing but
atoms remained of anything that ran afoul of it.

By the same token the source of the disruption
could be something that was planted to provide signals or a guidance beam for incoming space travelers.
If so, again I can conceive of many strange phenomena occurring when it was set off by accident or
even by design.

I had found indications of phenomena that went far beyond ordinary electromagnetic interference. The ocean looked different. Careful seamen, airmen, and pilots became irrational. Something, some force or intellect beyond anything yet known to our civilization, must have been operative from time to time in the Bermuda Triangle.

Certain other strange forces—one of them rather similar, apparently, to the unknown force in the Triangle—have been noted in Egypt. To find out what I could about them, I went there next.

# IX

## *Who Taught the Egyptians?*

I was flying east, looking for sites where my postulated earth colony might have established additional
bases. Engrossed in the detail of the hunt, I realized
that I had missed an obvious and startling principle.
According to virtually every expert, modern civilization had spread from east to west. My search was taking me in the opposite direction, counter to accepted
historical precedent. It was a lonely place to be, but
rewarding in the sense that if I were wrong, I was
wrong in a big way.

I had time on the flight to review the outlines of
data about advanced societies that flourished in the
Middle East almost six thousand years ago. I was particularly taken by Sumer.

Where did the Sumerians of Mesopotamia come
from? They pop up like some devilish jack-in-the-box,
around 3000 B.C., fully equipped with the first written
language, sophisticated mathematics, a knowledge of
physics, chemistry, and medicine. If their origins were
puzzling, their disappearance as a united society two
thousand years later was equally disturbing. As I
tried to unravel the story, I found myself building a
skeletal framework of surmise.

My time frame was fifty-thousand years. At some
point in that scale I had supposed that there was an
infusion of extraterrestrial colonists, possessed of technology advanced well beyond our own today. They
settled on pinpoints of the Earth, using their own

skills and capabilities to create the necessities of survival. The fragile seed took root. A handful of generations passed. And then came one of Earth's frequent cataclysmic events. The young colonies were ravaged. Perhaps the best and the brightest of their number were shuttled off the planet to continue their quest for a new home in safer parts of the universe. What was left were fragments of a highly advanced culture struggling for survival. Here and there were tiny pockets, slivers of humanity possessed of great knowledge but lacking the wherewithal to regenerate an elaborate technology.

It seemed to me that they might have faced a situation comparable to the story of the airplane that crash-landed in 1972 on a Chilean mountain peak. The passsengers survived, but in subsequent efforts to sustain themselves, they made little or no use of the wrecked plane as a source of material to create tools, weapons, or other accouterments that might be helpful. Within a short time they reverted to cannibalism in order to live. Could that have been the fate of Earth colonies struck by cataclysm?

My picture now was almost complete in outline. Instead of a straight upward line of development to modern man I had fashioned the possibility of an advanced beginning followed by setback, followed in turn by new advancement as the course of man's progress. The idea helped place into perspective all the oddments of information I had been accumulating. Perhaps the surprising accomplishments I had seen were part of a carry-over from earlier times. They were derived from knowledge somehow retained or mechanical devices imitated in their crudest forms as vestigial memories of the descendants of those first colonists.

Somewhere in Sumer with its strange beginnings and ancient Egypt with its marvelous advancements I hoped to find further verification of the theory. In my quest of something that might have lain waiting in Egypt through the millennia, I decided to go first to Saqqara.

Twenty miles below Cairo on the Nile is what is

left of Memphis, the most ancient of Egypt's capitals. Where two dynasties of pharaohs had ruled I now saw nothing but a row of small pyramids and a grove of palms. For the rest there was only desert.

Infinite, irritating sand, slipping into the boots, stinging the eyes, filling the pores, covering everything, stretching from Morocco across Sinai, Arabia, Turkestan, Tibet, to Mongolia. Along that sandy belt across two continents, civilization had once built splendid cities but now was gone—driven away, as the ice receded, by soaring temperatures and dwindling rainfall.

By the Nile, for a dozen miles on either side, I could see a ribbon of green growths. From the Mediterranean to Nubia there was only this strip redeemed from the desert. This was the thread on which ancient Egypt's life hung.

In the solitude of open desert, I walked through the whispering palm grove where Memphis used to be, and beyond it I glimpsed the gleaming white walls of Saqqara. Its simple elegance attracted me. Saqqara was scaled for human beings, not for giants.

On previous trips to Egypt I had felt a bit repelled by the heavy ornate grandeur of Giza and Karnak. They were built around awesome deserted temples. I had walked down imposing silent avenues of aloof blank-eyed statues. I had looked at walls covered with art that seemed flat and static.

I had never felt any kinship to people who had made those buildings and pictures—nor to the austere Pharaoh Khafre in the Cairo Museum, nor to Queen Hatshepsut masquerading as Osiris in the Metropolitan Museum. But at Saqqara I felt an aura of more likeable people.

Its stone buildings had the clean handsome lines that today's architects try to put into skyscrapers. Its corridor of ribbed pillars suggested the columns of classic Greece—although Greeks would not build temples until at least two thousand years later.

I could imagine that Saqqara's grace had been the product of generations of refinement—of architects, sculptors, and painters who were so wise and sophisticated that they had outgrown the taste for ornate architecture. And yet I knew that almost the opposite was the fact.

Saqqara was not the product of Egypt's mature or declining centuries. It was built by a young nation that arose out of squabbling tribes and suddenly began to create the world's first monumental architecture in stone.

Saqqara was built in the seminal era that started about 2700 B.C. and ushered in Egypt's first golden age of peace and prosperity, known as the Old Kingdom. This was an age of almost unbelievable inventiveness. It produced Egypt's first and finest pyramids, as well as some of its loveliest art—and set the shape of many things to come for the next three thousand years. Saqqara was to be a holy place all through subsequent Egyptian history.

Before the Old Kingdom, the scattered tribes that shared the Nile lived partly by fishing, partly by simple agriculture. They were just beginning to replace stone with metal tools. But something happened. Unexpectedly, almost mysteriously, they decided to cooperate in holding back the river's annual flood so that all could reap abundant harvests.

Cooperation meant organization. A semilegendary organizer named Narmer was credited with unifying Egypt and founding its first royal dynasty. The newly unified nation shot from Stone Age culture to an original and brilliant civilization.

As I read its history, it seemed to me that the civilization didn't evolve, it just occurred. Tools, techniques, architecture, engineering, medicine, science, and well-organized big cities materialized within a century or two—almost as if they had been imported from somewhere else.

I went to Saqqara because I wondered if the early Egyptians had received an "infusion of civilization" from one or more ancient astronauts. I soon became aware that the first real person in known history was the teacher of those who built Saqqara.

He was a remarkable genius named Imhotep—not a conqueror or king but an artist and scientist. The

WHO TAUGHT THE EGYPTIANS? 91

world's first known architect and engineer, he was also an administrator and healer of the sick. Posterity made him a god. Could he have come from outer space?

At Saqqara I saw visible evidence of what he did. Saqqara's artisans were apparently among the first, anywhere in the world, to master the difficult techniques of creating large, handsome stone buildings. The highly sophisticated construction was done by people who had known no better building material than sunbaked bricks a century earlier. The records showed that Imhotep taught them.

He was the grand vizier (prime minister) of the second pharaoh of the Old Kingdom. Imhotep was one of the very, very few in Egypt's well-filled pantheon who was promoted from mortal to deity. Egyptologists of the last century were skeptical about his human origins. At that time the only information they had about him was found in accounts written two and one-half millennia after his presumed lifetime.

There was, for example, the terse statement in a history of the pharaohs by Manetho, an Egyptian priest who lived in the third century before Christ and wrote in Greek. Manetho noted that "during the reign of Zoser I, lived Imhotep, who was the inventor of the art of building with hewn stone. He also improved the writing."

The Greeks knew Imhotep, at least by reputation, under the name Imouthes. They identified him with their god of medicine, Aesculapius. He was also the patron demigod of scribes and bureaucrats; both Greek and Egyptian scribes, when they mixed water with lampblack to make ink, poured out the last drop as a libation in Imhotep's honor.

In 1926 archaeologists established once and for all that Imhotep had been a living man, not just a legend. A statue of the pharaoh Zoser was dug out of the sand around Saqqara. On the base of it were Imhotep's name and his titles. The honor of being mentioned on a statue was rare in a land where all great works were routinely credited to the pharaoh. So Egyptologists at last felt justified in saying authoritatively that Imhotep, not Zoser, was responsible for raising the first great stone building on earth, the Step Pyramid at Saqqara. Leonard Cottrell, archaeological writer, called the Step Pyramid "the oldest, most awe-inspiring monumental stone structure in the world."

Another famous archaeologist, Jean-Philippe Lauer, once said of this pyramid: "When I realized its importance—the first building in the world to be built of cut stone in level courses, and designed by Imhotep, the Michelangelo of the age—I decided then to consecrate myself to this work." He gave the next forty-two years of his life to the task of reconstructing, stone by stone, the thirty-seven-acre temple complex surrounding the Step Pyramid. The result became one of the breathtaking sights of Egypt.

I walked along a magnificent wall, thirty-four feet high and more than a mile long, that enclosed the complex. Inside the wall I saw the pharaoh's open court for ceremonial sprints. I saw limestone columns carved in graceful plant designs, carved ceiling simulating wooden roofing logs, and carved walls made to resemble the reed matting that covered the walls of Egyptian houses. All this was a handsome duplicate in stone of the mud-brick palace and temples and enclosures that once served the pharaoh in his earthly capital at Memphis.

Dwarfing them was the pyramid. It was 413 feet by 344 feet at the base, a guide told me, and it soared skyward in six giant terraces for almost 200 feet. I entered it by walking down a colonnade with fluted columns, and then through ponderous stone doors. Those doors, perpetually ajar, reproduced down to the last details the wooden doors of early palace architecture.

Inside, I followed a long sloping corridor until I found myself looking down into a pit ninety feet deep. At the bottom lay the granite-walled burial room with a hole in the top to admit Zoser's body—the hole once sealed by a granite plug weighing several tons.

From this chamber many corridors branched out.

They led down and down, a hundred feet under the sandy surface of the Sahara, to where rooms had been carved out of the solid rock. "What were their purposes?" I asked. Nobody knew.

One room was still lined with green blue glazed tile panels imitating reed mats that might once have adorned the rooms of Zoser's palace. If the rooms had any peculiar powers, I didn't discern them. But I couldn't help remembering that the larger pyramids, modeled on this one, supposedly had only one or two chambers inside them. If this archetype contained many rooms, maybe there were more rooms in the other pyramids than had yet been discovered.

Authorities agreed that the Step Pyramid truly was the prototype of the much bigger pyramids, built of mighty ten-ton blocks, that would arise at Giza within the next two centuries. If the pyramid and the temple complex around it were Imhotep's only achievements, he would still be remembered, for they opened a splendid thousand-year epoch in architecture.

But Imhotep, in addition to being a pioneer architect, was a statesman, astronomer, priest—and above all a physician.

The glory of young Egypt's science was medicine. Apparently Imhotep was the nation's first and most gifted medical man. Later ages credited him with divine power to heal the sick.

Ancient writings described a great sanctuary he had outside Memphis—a combination of temple and sanatorium that was the Lourdes of ancient Egypt. It was called the Asclepieion because Greek settlers in Egypt named it after their own god of medicine.

Here flocked the sick to be cured, the crippled to be reshaped, the sterile to become fertile. Egyptians, Greeks, the Romans who succeeded the Greeks as masters of Egypt—all came to implore Imhotep's help, and kept coming for centuries.

The place also contained a medical school run by Imhotep's disciples. Fledgling doctors got their essential professional training there. Never before, as far as I could find out, was any kind of professional training given anywhere in the world.

To judge from ancient narratives, some sort of magic was part of the training of those at the Asclepieion. The literature of Egypt was full of magicians—of wizards who caused severed limbs to grow back in place, or who raised the dead. Here is one account of an incident at the hospital, written by an anonymous Greek who went there to be treated:

> I was burning up with a violent fever and convulsed with loss of breath and coughing because of the pain in my side. My head was heavy from my suffering, and I was dropping off half-conscious into sleep.
>
> My mother was sitting distraught at my torment. Suddenly she spied—it was no dream or sleep, for her eyes were fixed wide open—a divine apparition.
>
> It came in, terrifying her.
>
> All she could see was that there was someone of more than human height, clothed in shining garments and holding in his left hand a book. He merely eyed me two or three times from head to foot and then disappeared.
>
> Finding me drenched with sweat but with my fever completely gone, she knelt down in worship to the divine manifestation. After these pains in my side had ceased, and the god had given me one more healing treatment, I proclaimed his benefactions to all.

I wondered how an Egyptian priest arranged for superhuman stature and shining garments. I wondered how he broke fevers or cured pains in the side. No writings from the Asclepieion survived. Even its exact location became unknown.

But there seemed no doubt that Egyptian medicine was at the roots of modern western medicine. Hippocrates, father of medicine in the fifth century B.C., admitted a debt to Egypt. I found several scholarly books that said that medical science began there.

They said, for example, that Egypt had great physicians, surgeons, and specialists. Some were obstetricians or gynecologists. Some treated only gastric disorders. Some were oculists so internationally famous that Cyrus sent for one to come to Persia. Clay tablets found at Tel el 'Amarna showed that Egyptian medical men were often sent to foreign courts in Syria and Assyria. They were antiquity's equivalent of the first Viennese psychoanalysts.

Several papyruses devoted to medicine were handed down to us. The most valuable, named for the Edwin Smith who discovered it, is an undated and anonymous roll fifteen feet long. It is the oldest medical textbook known to history—and it deals with its subject in a rational way, with no nonsense about charms or incantations.

It describes forty-eight cases in clinical surgery, from skull fractures to spinal injuries. Each case is treated in logical order, under the heads of provisional diagnosis, examination, diagnosis, prognosis, treatment—and even footnotes on the terms used.

The anatomist Warren Dawson pointed out that this papyrus showed that Egyptians had studied the brain, and knew somehow that injury to it would affect other parts of the body. Treatment explained in the papyrus included reducing dislocations, healing fractures by the use of splints and casts, and closing open wounds with sutures, clamps, or some unknown kind of adhesive plaster. How could such a young civilization acquire so much medical knowledge so quickly?

More amazing yet, Egyptian doctors' herbal prescriptions were so prized that they spread all over the Mediterranean area. They knew seven hundred medicines, for everything from snakebite to puerperal fever. This was no exaggerated legend. The medicines are listed in another early document, the Ebers Papyrus.

Even today we still trustfully swallow many strange mixtures that were brewed four thousand years ago on the banks of the Nile. Among drugs recommended by ancient Egyptian doctors and pharmacists, and still used today, are acacia, anise, castor beans (good old castor oil was a laxative for Egyptians), coriander, saffron, and wormwood. Mineral substances they used in medicine included arsenic, alum, niter (of which the very name was Egyptian), sodium bicarbonate, and sulfur.

Whether or not Imhotep personally brought this medical knowledge to Egypt, the Egyptians certainly revered him as the greatest healer of all time. Hundreds of bronze statuettes of him—probably votives offered by grateful worshipers—were unearthed by Egyptologists. The Louvre alone has fifty.

These statuettes show him not as a god but as a learned man with clean-shaven head, sometimes covered with a skullcap, wearing an apron and sandals, sitting meditatively with an open scroll on his lap. They date back to about the sixth century B.C. Not until three centuries later did Imhotep become Egypt's god of medicine. The likenesses of him made around 300 B.C. show him standing, like most Egyptian deities, complete with beard, scepter, and a symbol of life and happiness. Temples to worship Imhotep were built from the marshes of the delta to the sands of Nubia.

It would be logical to expect that such a revered and powerful man would be buried in a tomb almost as splendid as those of the pharaohs. Apparently he wasn't, and that's peculiar.

What distinguished Egypt's religion above everything else was its emphasis on immortality. Since the Nile, Osiris, and all vegetation could rise again, so could man. The amazing preservation of dead bodies in the dry sand of Egypt lent some encouragement to this belief, which was to dominate Egyptian faith for thousands of years—and which was to pass by its own resurrection into Christianity.

To an Egyptian, life on earth was just a prelude to an eternal existence in the hereafter that duplicated the best moments of his mortal career. This he would spend in his spacious tomb. So it had to be no mere monument or mausoleum but a fully equipped home—and, for a noble such as Imhotep, one that was commensurate with his station. The grand vizier of a pharaoh undoubtedly would be laid to rest in one of the grandest tombs. And, just as surely, his burial place would turn out to be not merely a tomb but the nucleus of a vast complex.

Strangely, however, no tomb was ever found for Imhotep.

Practically every archaeologist who worked near Saqqara searched in vain for it. One or two devoted decades almost exclusively to the quest. They scanned all existing Egyptian writings for some clue.

But they never found even a mention of his death.

Do you see what I was wondering? Could Imhotep have been one of those man-gods like Viracocha, Quetzalcoatl, Kukulcán—and perhaps Jesus—who possessed great wisdom and seemingly miraculous powers, and who just "went away" instead of dying and being buried?

I never found out. After so many thousands of years, I could hardly hope to solve the mystery of Imhotep's phenomenal knowledge and eventual disappearance (if he did disappear). But by the time I'd finished absorbing all the information I could gather about him, I was willing to consider the possibility that some of his works would still be thought either magical or faked if they were performed in our own time.

The Egyptian priests had exceptional, perhaps unique, opportunities to learn and pass along whatever hidden knowledge Imhotep might have brought with him. They acquired a formidable reputation as magicians, seers, powerful wise men, throughout the ancient world—a reputation often recognized and acknowledged by the Greeks, who were no fools.

The priests themselves had a legend that their knowledge had come from Thoth, the god of wisdom, during his three-thousand-year reign on earth. Thoth was associated somehow with the moon, the priests said. The images they made of him showed him not with a human head but with the head of an ibis, the bird venerated by Imhotep—and conceivably a symbol for a man who wore a space helmet. Could the legend of Thoth have filtered down from a visit by some benign supernatural being? I remembered how GI Joe had become a generic wartime term for American soldiers who cheerfully scattered gifts and friendship in Europe, Japan, and Southeast Asia. Had "Thoth," descending from the skies to bring mankind knowledge, become a collective name for spacemen?

I knew people interested in occult studies who claimed that Thoth was an Atlantean who helped build the Great Pyramid, and secreted inside it tablets of wisdom and magical tools. To the Egyptians he was a supreme god-of-all trades.

This learned deity supposedly composed the most ancient Egyptian books, which the priests said were "in the very handwriting of the god." Writing was one of his inventions. A legend related that when Thoth revealed the art of writing to King Thamos, the good king denounced it as a threat to society. "Children and young people who had hitherto been forced to apply themselves, to learn and retain whatever was taught them, would neglect to exercise their memories, and cease to apply themselves," the monarch protested.

Whether or not Thoth (or Imhotep) taught them, the priests were apparently the first men on earth who could write. And from somewhere they had learned to make paper, by flattening and drying the pith of the papyrus reed. Then they went on to establish scribal schools adjacent to the temples. A new class of literate men grew up to be the civil servants and administrators of the newly united kingdom.

If the priests who served Imhotep were capable of all this, I thought, conceivably they were capable of other feats that never became known to later generations.

The best surviving evidence of what they knew was, perhaps, the pyramids. I was determined to find out more about those astounding structures before leaving Egypt.

# X

## *Secrets in Stone*

Some psychic mediums and sensitives have insisted they felt magnetic force around certain Egyptian pyramids. The first scientist to suspect that some kind of electromagnetic discharge was pumping from the interior of a pyramid was Dr. Louis Alvarez, a Nobel Prize winner in physics.

Archaeologists had long wondered whether there were any undiscovered secret chambers in the big Second Pyramid, built for the Pharaoh Khafre at Giza. (Of about seventy-five pyramids that Egypt is known to have built during its long history, the Second Pyramid was one of the four most famous.) Five years ago Dr. Alvarez devised an elaborate array of electronic devices to probe the pyramid.

He planned to make use of a mysterious radiation of energy from space, first discovered in 1911 by the Austrian physicist Victor Hess on balloon flights high in the atmosphere. Dr. Robert Millikan, who collected a great store of information on this radiation—and gave it the name "cosmic rays"—decided that it must be a form of electromagnetic radiation. It could pass through almost anything, even several feet of lead.

This penetrating power was what Dr. Alvarez intended to use at Giza. Deep inside the pyramid, he set up his electronic devices to record the cosmic rays passing through it. The equipment soundings were transcribed on tapes, which were then run through a computer programmed to create a "picture" of the pyramid interior, like an X-ray photograph.

But to everyone's bewilderment the computer balked.

Dr. Amr Gonied, who was in charge of the project at the IBM data center in Cairo, reported that the computer was spewing out nonsensical diagrams of the pyramid's measurements. Yet the computer functioned perfectly in all other projects it was being used on at the same time. IBM technicians checked it thoroughly and found it in perfect working order.

This meant that Dr. Gonied must be feeding it garbage, as computer people would say. In other words, something was wrong with the tapes from the cosmic ray soundings of the pyramid.

Dr. Alvarez never discovered exactly what the trouble was. He eventually gave up, because the cosmic-ray counter continued to go awry whenever he tried to use it inside the pyramid. He has wondered ever since whether something sealed inside that mountainous stone structure is still at work, emitting (or attracting?) some sort of rays or waves.

A few other investigators noticed oddities that made them wonder too. A Frenchman named Bovis, visiting the King's Chamber of the Great Pyramid with a party of tourists, got curious because the litter left there by hordes of visitors didn't seem to give off the unpleasant smells that most trash does. He poked through the pile and found that it included some dead kittens; even these had no smell of putrefaction, in spite of the stuffy air in the chamber. He took the cadavers away with him, dissected them, and found them so dehydrated that they were mummified. What had happened to them in the King's Chamber? He had no idea. The Egyptians had kept mummies in stone coffins but no mummy has ever been found entombed in a pyramid.

His peculiar discovery came to the ears of a Czechoslovakian radio engineer, Karel Drbal, who was intrigued enough to devise some tests of his own. Drbal built small models of pyramids and found "a definite relation between the shape of the space inside the pyramid and the physical, chemical and biological processes going on inside the space."

Pursuing this further, he made an exact miniature of the Great Pyramid and put a razor blade inside it, just to see what would happen.

He knew of the old legends that the pyramid had once contained such fabulous materials as glass that would bend without breaking and swords that would not rust. And his miniature pyramid eventually produced a puzzling phenomenon that brought him considerable wealth.

When he placed the razor blade one-third of the way to the top of his little pyramid, about where the King's Chamber is in the Great Pyramid, and aligned his mini pyramid squarely with true north as the Great Pyramid is, his blade became virtually immune not only to rusting but to dulling. Each morning he took it out, got a close shave with it, and reinserted it in his pyramid. He found that it stayed sharp for more than a hundred shaves.

He made other models of the pyramid and found that they had the same effect on razor blades. So he went into the business of making and selling small styrofoam pyramids. His patented device is known as the Cheops Razor Blade Sharpener in European countries, and as the Toth Pyramid in this country. Alert entrepreneurs picked up Drbal's concept in France and Italy, producing pyramid-shaped milk and yogurt cartons that definitely retarded spoilage. Nobody can explain why or how pyramidal structures have this effect. Apparently the ancient Egyptians knew something we don't.

As I traveled out through the desert toward the Great Pyramid, for mile after mile I saw men digging deep holes in the sand, patiently carrying away the subsoil in little paired baskets slung over the shoulder on a pole. A pith-helmeted Egyptologist was bending absorbed over hieroglyphics on two stones just rescued from the earth. He was one of a thousand such men, living simply in the heat and dust, trying to read the riddles of the Sphinx and ferret out the history and wisdom of Egypt. There were fifty-nine separate archaeological projects in progress along the Nile when I arrived. This wasn't unusual. Year in and year out, men had been magnetized by the ruins of old Egypt.

Nearly twenty-five hundred years ago, during a trip to Egypt, the Greek traveler and historian Herodotus set down his amazement at what he had seen in that already ancient land. "There is no country that has so many wonders," he said.

Even then the pyramids were at least twenty centuries old, as remote to him as the Acropolis is now to us. I knew, not only from his writings but from other evidence, that in his day the pyramids were visited by strings of tourists, special sorts of priests acting as guides. The graffiti those pre-Christian sightseers scribbled on the walls were still visible to me. Many had been deciphered and published.

As I steeped myself in the atmosphere of the valley of the Nile, I thought how much had happened here. Egypt was rich in art and accomplishment when Europe was in its Stone Age. It was about to start its last great flowering when the ancestors of Homer's heroes were semibarbarians in battle on the ringing plains of windy Troy. Egypt was a prize for Alexander when he conquered all his worlds.

The lure of this empire on the edge of a dreary sand-blown desert, I mused, had been one of the facts of our world throughout recorded history. The Hebrews, the Greeks, and the Romans were much impressed by ancient Egypt, and some of them paid respectful credit to it for its learning and skill. Its mysteries, its treasures, the stupendous debris of its vanished world magnetized men in every age. Much of the time they came in ignorance and for profit, dragging carved granite away by the ton to adorn museums or collections abroad. The pyramids served for many centuries as a convenient stone quarry for local builders. The mass plundering ended less than a century ago.

After that a different breed began to swarm around Cairo—just as single-minded, but driven by a desire to learn rather than to loot. Camped in the desert for

# FASCINATING CLUES TO THE MYSTERIES OF THE ORIGIN OF MAN

The planet Earth
as seen by the crew
of Apollo 17. Was
this the same view seen
by ancient astronauts
13,000 years ago?

1 Entrance to the Tiahuanaco temple. Tiahuanaco is the city
that predates all known history of the Peruvian Andes.
Located on a plateau 13,000 feet above sea level, the
entrance is all that remains of an enormous
structure that took an estimated 100,000 people to build.
The region surrounding the temple shows no evidence
of land capable of supporting crops or livestock.

2 The Monolith. Weighing more than twenty tons, the
carving of a god is duplicated in many forms
throughout Central and South America. The helmet-like
cap and the strange device attached to the chest
are of particular interest since they would seem to indicate
an orientation toward a space-suited figure.

<sup>3</sup> Gate of the Sun. A twelve- by ten-foot rock
slab through which an entrance has been carved. The
decorations on the Gate of the Sun display the
weeping gods. Most authorities consider the structure
to be a complex astronomical calendar.

4 The Sunken Wall. The massive pieces of rock
that form the wall carvings were made in prehistoric
times representing every race on earth. Examples
of Caucasian, Negroid, Asiatic and Semitic features
are visible in the individual close-ups. How
could these cultures have been known to the carvers?

⁵ Sacsahuamán, showing what appears to be a
snake-like carving in a rock. By legend warriors received
great powers by putting their hand inside the
"snake's head." A compass put inside the head spins crazily,
indicating extraordinary electromagnetic forces.

6 Ollantaytambo, a pre-Incan fortress. Each boulder weighs
from twelve to one hundred tons. They were transported
from a mountaintop seven miles from Ollantaytambo
without the benefit of a wheel, down into a valley, across
a rushing river and back up a second mountainside.

7 The calendar of Sacsahuamán. Light
alternately fills the empty squares in the outer
ring marking each hour of the day.

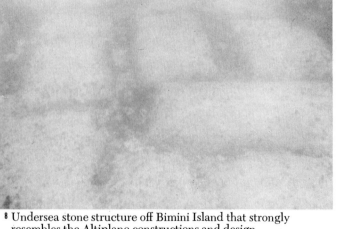

8 Undersea stone structure off Bimini Island that strongly
resembles the Altiplano constructions and design.
Could this have been another base for ancient visitors?

⁹ City planning, Incan style, carved in a boulder.

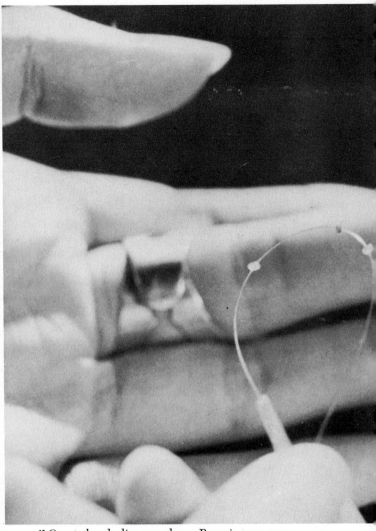

10 Quartz beads discovered on a Peruvian mummy.
The holes that have been drilled in the quartz could not have
been made by any known commercial drill in existence today.

11 Spaceman carved in gold.

12 Among the same pre-Incan
gold carvings there is a figure
that definitely resembles the
designs of a delta-wing jet fighter.

13 The Iron Pillar outside New Delhi, that dates
to 1500 B.C., is made of an alloy that will not rust.
Even today we cannot duplicate the alloy.

<sup>14</sup> Computer parts dating from 50 B.C.?
The only explanation for the existence of the
mechanical wheels displayed here is the
probability that they were part of a digital computer.

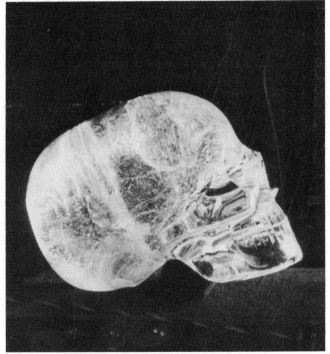

15 Crystal skull. The amazing detail on the crystal
  skull, which is dated at approximately 200,000 B.C.,
  could not have been made by any known
  tool in existence at the time it was created.

16 A printing device, perhaps 1,000 A.D., found in the Andes that prints Egyptian-like figures.

17 Babylonian tablet describing
spacemen arriving on earth. There
is also an Indian text which
gives explicit descriptions for
building an airplane.

18 San Torini, an example of a city that was apparently
evacuated in an extraordinarily orderly manner. Apparently
they knew of the onslaught of a volcanic cataclysm
and left, taking all of their valuables but leaving the normal
materials of life behind. Is this Atlantis?

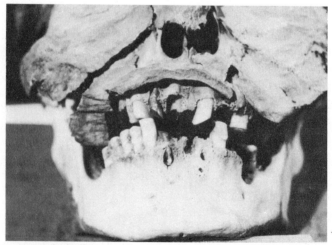

19 Inca man's skull, approximately 700 years
old, mummified with two false teeth in place.
No parallel in historical dentistry.

**20** The astronomical observatory at New Delhi
has a staircase to nowhere. An explanation for the
staircase is that it was part of a physical
observation platform which lined up exactly with
the North star and is part of the astronomical
alignment theory outlined in the book.

21 Dead Sea Scrolls, Israel, and the cave
entrance where they were found.

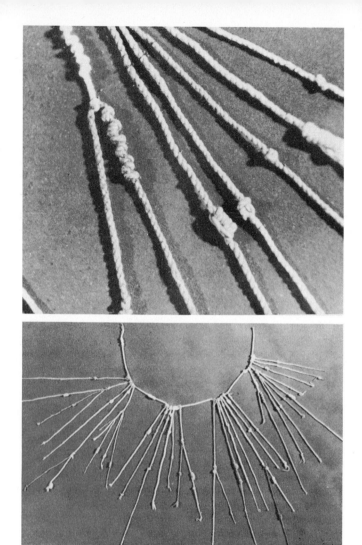

²²Inca "Quipu" string computer, used for calculation
in their society, which never had a written language.

23 Petroglyph; drawing of a spaceman done by
American Indians at China Lake, California.

<sup>24</sup> Space suited figurine.

<sup>25</sup> Australian bark painting; "Wodjina,"
goddess of the outback.

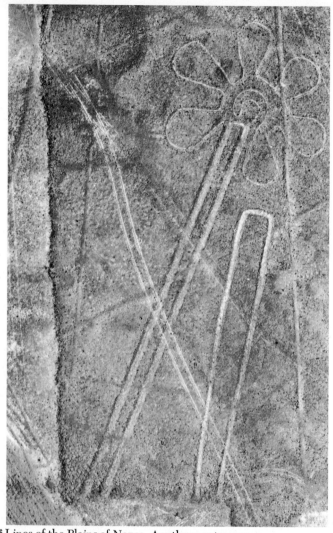

26 Lines of the Plains of Nazca. Are they route-map
indicators for space visitors, oriented by a
3-mile line that marks the summer solstice?

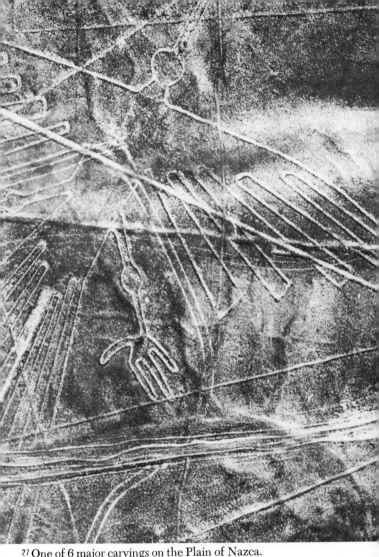

27 One of 6 major carvings on the Plain of Nazca.
A hovering hummingbird, a figure associated
throughout mythology with the arrival of gods.

28 Bay of Pisco, a three-prong indicator of the
direction toward the Plains of Nazca. This is more
than 2,000 years old, of unknown origin.

months on end, digging, measuring, copying, restoring, collecting, classifying, interpreting, four generations of Egyptologists gradually pieced together the panorama of Egyptian life.

And the great search was still gaining momentum while I was there. Exciting finds were being made. Archaeologists were using sophisticated new tools in addition to the traditional picks and shovels, knives and trowels and camel's hair brushes. They were experimenting with the computer and the cosmic-ray counter, as I mentioned earlier. Similarly, airborne infrared sensors were bringing back ghostly pictures of the past, revealing subterranean outlines of vanished buildings, canals, bridges, dams. (One Apollo photo of the Nile Delta, for example, enabled cartographers to locate and label more than a thousand native villages that no map had shown.) Other spectographic sensors in satellites were able to glance down at a pile of rock and tell its approximate age, its mineral makeup, the cavities hidden within it, the external forces that had been at work on it. However, for the moment it seemed more important for the satellites to gather data for ecologists rather than archaeologists.

Everything found in Egypt so far, according to the veteran British archaeologist Walter Emery, was "only a small fraction of what still lies hidden beneath the sands."

For me, the pyramids were still Egypt's most provocative objects of study.

Built of stone blocks that weighed up to fifteen tons, yet that fitted together with the precision of a necklace clasp, they apparently had required decades of toil by many thousands of workmen. What under heaven inspired a few pharaohs to build in a way never equaled before or since? What was in Egyptian minds when they made those fortresslike monuments, when they constructed artfully hidden entrances with blind doors, and dead-end passages ending hard up against impenetrable granite blocks? If protection against grave robbers were the only object, there were quicker ways to achieve the same ends. Why

should a pharaoh raise a veritable geometric mountain of stone over his sarcophagus?

Swallowing the tall tales of local guides, Herodotus
reported that one-hundred thousand slaves had toiled
for twenty years on the Great Pyramid. And I knew
from my reading that, until fairly recently, Egyptologists had believed him. It was taken for granted that
the gigantic work could only have been done by armies of forced labor.

This assumption, made against Egypt's backdrop of
silent tombs and colossal monuments, gave scholars a
vision of a gloomy people, preoccupied by thoughts of
death and forever hauling huge blocks under the cutting whips of the overseers.

But I had seen newer evidence proving that this
was a false picture. Only about four thousand construction workers were used at a time. They were free
citizens drafted for public works during the off-season
when the Nile floods kept them from working in the
fields. They were well fed; old records show amazing
quantities of radishes, onions, and garlic brought in to
season the workmen's meals.

Men toiled in gangs of eighteen or twenty, hauling
the heavy stone blocks up ramps and setting them in
place. On many pyramid blocks the quarry gangs
pridefully wrote the names of their outfits in red
ocher: "Vigorous Gang," or "Enduring Gang."

The work was surely no picnic, I thought, but almost certainly there were times when pyramid building for a god-king had some of the elation of cathedral building in the Middle Ages. Some gangs were
so pleased to work for the pharaoh that, as a foreman
recorded, they toiled "without a single man getting
exhausted, without a man thirsting," and at last "came
home in good spirits, sated with bread, drunk with
beer, as if it were the beautiful festival of a god." So I
knew that, far from being morbid or oppressed, the
Egyptians of the pyramid-building age were sociable
and lighthearted, and among the most industrious of
ancient peoples.

For many centuries the pyramids were presumed to
have been meant only as tombs for the pharaohs who

had them built. But recent generations have gazed on their awesome massiveness, and wondered. Some people felt intuitively that the pyramids must have served some higher purpose than as mere tombstones. So the studies expanded.

A small desert plateau near the village of Giza "may well claim to be the most remarkable piece of ground in the world," in the opinion of the dean of scientific archaeologists, Sir William Matthew Flinders Petrie.

He was referring to the ground where the three largest pyramids were built: the Great Pyramid attributed to Khufu (Cheops) and two somewhat smaller ones for other pharaohs. "There," Petrie wrote, "may be seen the very beginnings of architecture, the most enormous piles of buildings ever raised, the most accurate construction known, the finest masonry, and the employment of the most ingenious tools."

As engineering achievements these pyramids were wonderful enough without attributing any mysterious functions to them. Considering when they were built, and the tools and materials the Egyptians worked with, they had to be the most difficult constructions ever conceived by man.

I could grant that our huge concrete dams and steel suspension bridges were technologically more advanced and—to our civilization—more useful. But it still seemed to me that our engineers, able and dedicated as they are, deserve less credit than the pyramid builders because they work with ready-mixed concrete, structural steel, explosives for blasting, and powered machines for lifting.

How well would they do if they had to duplicate one of Egypt's pyramids with no metal tools but primitive copper chisels and hammers; no surveying instruments but strings, bits of charcoal, and the stars; no means of moving two-ton stones but wedges, levers, sleds, palm-fiber ropes, and rafts?

The great feats of pyramid building, requiring smooth teamwork as well as the most precise and logical calculations, implied a profound fact about Egypt expressed by Rudolf Anthes: "When all is said and done, Egyptian history suggests that about 3000 B.C. religious and logical matters of thinking were in better balance than they were about 1000 B.C. in Egypt, or in the present-day world. The early Egyptians employed reason in the highest degree when it was called for, and approached with due reverence what was beyond their thinking."

All Egyptian dates before 663 B.C. were only approximations, I knew; Egyptologists amused themselves by moving the earlier ones up and down by centuries. Nevertheless, whatever the date, I could see evidence that mathematical knowledge was well developed at the very outset of recorded Egyptian history. The design of the pyramids implied an expertise that was impossible without a broad mathematical background. Nearly all the ancients agreed in ascribing the invention of this science to the Egyptians.

Likewise, I suspected that the Egyptians knew more astronomy than some authorities gave them credit for. They knew enough to predict the day on which the Nile would rise, and to "orient" many of their structures—that is to say, to build the same sort of temple so that the shrine and entrance always faced in the same direction, usually east.

The Sphinx faced due east. Some temples faced the exact point where the sun would rise on the morning of the summer solstice. Others pointed north, and others again pointed to the rising of the star Sirius or to the rising point of other conspicuous stars.

I wondered if the priests knew more than they cared to publish among a people whose superstitions were so precious to their rulers. From the earliest prehistory men had gazed at the night sky and wondered. Astronomy was probably the first pure science. Either the astronomers were given a head start by a superintelligence somewhere, or else they had spent endless nights of watching, generations of careful counting, in order to learn how the stars could help a traveler find his way, how they could tell farmers when to plant, when to prepare for harvest, when to expect colder or warmer months. It was the priests who foretold these events for the people, without explaining how they knew.

To the priests, the secret and mysterious study of astronomy was beginning to link the movements of heavenly bodies with the powers of shrine and temple. They were thinking about the gods they served and thinking new meanings into them. They were brooding on the mystery of the stars—partly, perhaps, because of faint faraway echoes of visitors from the stars?

For whatever reason, they would be inspired to keep studying. For century after century they were to keep track of the position and movements of the planets, until their records stretched back for thousands of years. They distinguished between planets and fixed stars, noted in their catalogs stars of the fifth magnitude (practically invisible to the unaided eye) and charted what they thought were the portents to mankind of the solemn silent movements of those shining bodies.

Recorded Egyptian history had barely begun when Zoser was laid to rest beneath Imhotep's Step Pyramid. Yet within the next seventy years or less the Great Pyramid was completed. Someone already knew a lot.

No authority would deny that this pyramid, even though it was simply a logical outgrowth of the Step Pyramid, did represent a spectacular advance both in use of materials and in sheer magnitude.

I got its exact dimensions and noted them down. It was about seven city blocks long on each side, along the base. When completed it had towered 481 feet, the height of a modern forty-story skyscraper.

More than two and one-quarter million stone blocks, weighing from four thousand to twenty-four thousand pounds each, yet hauled from hundreds of miles away, had gone into it. At least this was the closest estimate that Egyptologists could make without taking the pyramid apart to count and weigh its stones.

I had read that when the pyramid was completed it was sheathed in polished white limestone, and the apex was probably capped with gold, so that from miles away peasants in the fields or nomads crossing the desert could see the great symbol of superhuman power gleaming against the sky.

Superhuman power? Yes. Height and mass and resplendence weren't the most remarkable features of the Great Pyramid. Centuries later, men began to make surprising discoveries about it—discoveries that even now seemed impossible to explain.

The Copts first got outsiders curious about the interiors of the pyramids. The Copts were a Christian sect who traced their ancestry back to the ancient Egyptians, and who used a church language similar to Egyptian. (Egypt was Christianized from neighboring Palestine in the fourth and fifth centuries.) For centuries they met in secret lodges to honor the old gods of Egypt. A Coptic writer named Masudi, who lived in medieval times, wrote: "One of the kings of Egypt before the Flood . . . built two great pyramids. He also ordered the priests to deposit therein the total of their wisdom and their knowledge of different arts and sciences, for the benefit of those who could eventually understand them."

This curious statement finally came to the attention of the Arabs, when they conquered Egypt for Islam in the seventh century and happened to find the sacred Coptic text. They also heard rumors among Egyptian natives of a "secret treasure" sealed up inside the Great Pyramid.

The Arabs were avid not only for gold and precious stones but also for knowledge, especially of astronomy and geography. They combed the Middle East for scientific manuscripts by Greek, Roman, and Hindu authors, sometimes paying for translations by the weight of the manuscript in gold. Consequently the young Caliph Abdullah al-Ma'mun resolved to ransack the pyramid for whatever it contained, whether secret knowledge or great wealth.

He went to Giza with a small army of engineers and laborers. They carefully inspected the slanting faces of the pyramid, but found no door. So the caliph ordered his men to bore straight into the solid stonework. When their chisels blunted, the Arabs lighted fires and doused the heated blocks with vinegar until they cracked enough to be dislodged with battering rams.

Their search, while destructive, was unrewarding. They did break into a long passageway inside the pyramid, and followed it to the King's Chamber—where they found only an empty granite sarcophagus that gave off an eerie sound when struck. That was all. No treasure, no wondrous bendable and unbreakable glass, no unrusted arms, no manuscripts about art and sciences. The disappointed caliph went home to Baghdad.

At no time was any artifact other than ordinary building debris ever recovered from the Great Pyramid. To me, this fact seemed mysterious in itself. If robbers had made off with all its contents, as the academicians insisted, how had they gotten in and out? If they sealed up their exit, why did they bother?

Not until another conquest of Egypt—this time in 1798 by young Napoleon Bonaparte and his army—did anyone begin to realize what the true secrets of the Great Pyramid might be.

Militarily his expedition, which aimed to cut Britain's routes to India, was a failure. But archaeologically it was momentous. Napoleon was acutely aware that he was marching onto soil that occupied a special place in history.

It was in the valley of the Nile, he knew, that man had first created a great unified nation, had first devised political institutions to rule a widespread geographical area, had first organized governmental machinery to administer thousands of people, had first executed large-scale projects. (The dim old Tiahuanaco empire, of course, was completely lost to view at that time. It might or might not have been as advanced an empire as Egypt. And even today no one can be sure whether Egypt or Tiahuanaco was born first.)

Certainly it was in the valley of the Nile that man achieved a way of life that included not only work

and duty but leisure and grace, gaiety and sophistica-
tion, enduring art. Along with this way of life, Egyptian man created its natural counterpart, a secular
literature—essays on how to succeed in life, discus-
sions of the state of the world, short stories of adventure, songs of love.

Thus Napoleon had ample reason for the famous
words he spoke when addressing his soldiers before
the Battle of the Pyramids: "Soldiers, from the summit of yonder pyramids, forty centuries look down
upon you." I knew now that "forty centuries" was an
underestimate.

Foresightedly, Napoleon had organized an intellectual task force of 175 scientists, antiquarians, and
artists whose mission was to explore and study the
little-known land. Under their ministrations a picture
began to take shape—eventually detailed in the
thirty-six big volumes of the *Description de
l'Egypte*—of a vital people gifted with great skills.

The strangest part of that picture was its center-
piece, the Great Pyramid.

In undertaking to map Egypt, the French civil engineers chose the pyramid as a convenient point of
triangulation. It was certainly the highest and most
stupendous. (Napoleon, on first seeing it, estimated
that it contained enough building material to make a
wall ten feet high around most of France. Others in
his task force calculated that its stones would reach
two-thirds of the way around the world at the equator.)

As the cartographers studied their triangulation
points they noticed that the pyramid was oriented to
true north within a tiny fraction of a degree. Its east
face was lined up precisely with the polar axis of the
planet.

Later the cartographers found that the pyramid
stood exactly in the center of the land map of the
world—not the known world of 2575 B.C. but the en-
tire world. If you look at a modern flat map of the
world, you'll see what I mean. Giza is midway between the west coast of Mexico on the left and the
east coast of China on the right; between Norway's

North Cape at the top and Africa's Cape of Good Hope at the bottom. Mercator projections of the world show modern Cairo (and old Giza, a few miles away) at the intersection of the thirtieth parallels of longitude and latitude.

The only way the pyramid's planners could have picked its central position (unless this happened by pure chance) would have been to survey Earth from space, make a global map, project it flat, then draw meridians through the precise middle of the map's land surface.

Titillated by these incredible discoveries, scholars buckled down to study the pyramid in ever-finer detail—measuring, weighing, testing, analyzing their data cautiously. Year after year the work went on. The body of confirmed findings grew slowly. Even the more conservative and skeptical members of the academic Establishment sometimes allowed themselves to think that the Great Pyramid embodied an unaccountable knowledge of this planet and its relation to the universe. They had to admit that the pyramid's location, orientation, and dimensions matched up closely with the measurements and bearings of Earth as a whole. This could hardly be coincidence.

Whoever planned this pyramid knew, as the legends had said, how to make excellent charts of the stars with which to calculate longitude, and how to draw maps of the globe by which one could travel at will across its continents and oceans. The Great Pyramid was a scale model of the northern hemisphere, drawn on a precise fraction of the circumference of the globe.

Hence it must have served as an observatory, among other things. Somehow its builders knew that the world was round but flattened at the poles, which caused a degree of latitude to lengthen at the top and bottom of the planet; that it rotated in one day on an axis tilted 23.5 degrees to the ecliptic, causing night and day, and that this tilt caused the seasons; that Earth circled the sun once in a year of 365 and a fraction days. All these facts and dimensions had exact analogues in the dimensions and placement of the pyramid.

The designers must also have known that Earth's celestial North Pole described a slow circle around the pole of the ecliptic, making the constellations in the sky appear to "slip backward" (the precession of the equinoxes) and bring a new constellation of the zodiac behind the sun at the equinox approximately every twenty-two hundred years in a grand cycle of about twenty-six thousand years. These facts too were part of the internal measurements of the pyramid. But had the designers observed the stars for twenty-two hundred years? No one could imagine how they might have; only a few hundred years before the pyramid was built, the Egyptians had been primitive river tribes.

Not until many centuries after the pyramid was built would other civilizations become able to compute Earth's circumference and the rate at which it revolved. For me at least, it was hard to escape the notion that a far older civilization's emissaries had helped the Egyptians with astronomy and mathematics.

If so, these old ones must have decided that for knowledge to survive it would have to be on records so big as to be practically indestructible. The Great Pyramid fulfilled such a requirement.

You can't really comprehend the immensity of this Matterhorn of masonry until you have been boosted up and then been eased down its majestic but dilapidated northern slope. The steps are narrow, barely fifteen inches wide. And to make matters worse for tourists these steps are very high, about three feet. Each step is just a few inches higher than the average leg and knee can manage. Hence the prosperity of the white-robed haulers and boosters who help you up and hand you down for all the baksheesh they can wheedle out of you.

No wonder I felt tired but triumphant when I stood for the first time atop this mountainous creation, 451 feet above the desert. Because the blocks that formed the apex are no longer there, the top of the pyramid is now a level platform some 36 feet square. From there I could look down upon the Second Pyramid, the supposed tomb of Khafre.

For its outward size and elegant dimensions the ancients considered the Great Pyramid the greatest (as well as the oldest) of the seven wonders of the world. But the unknown interior, with its corridors, passageways, air shafts, Grand Gallery, and King's Chamber, was no less an architectural marvel.

When I explored it as thousands of tourists do, I followed a guide down the sixty-two-foot Descending Corridor, then on all fours into the cavernous mausoleum, and up a hundred crouching steps to the very heart of the pyramid. There was the Great Hall—153 feet long, with a ceiling 28 feet high. I moved on into an antechamber and finally into the pharaoh's funerary chamber itself, 137 feet above ground level. It was walled with granite.

The Egyptians had needed great engineering skill in designing these interior spaces to withstand the massive weight of stone above them. The Grand Gallery, for example, was built with a tiered, braced ceiling. (The gallery was a high, narrow, sloping tunnel that led to the vestibule of the King's Chamber.)

This gallery could have served as a kind of telescope with a fixed meridian. Through it, a series of observers along the inclined slope could have accurately noted the transit of heavenly bodies just as the modern astronomer sets his transit circle to a vertical meridian. By looking down the descending passage into a reflecting pool, an Egyptian astronomer could have seen the exact moment of a star's transit. The U.S. Naval Observatory uses this same system today; the daily transit of stars is noted to a split second by their reflection in a pool of mercury.

According to Richard A. Proctor, a British astronomer and author who wrote at the end of the nineteenth century, the Grand Gallery was "the most perfect observatory ever made till the telescopic art revealed a way of exact observation without those massive structures." Using the gallery, the ancient astronomers may have mapped the heliocentric, or sun-centered, pattern of our solar system several thousand years before Copernicus.

The inner design of the pyramid included two "burial chambers" that were left unfinished. Why?

The accepted theory among archaeologists is that the pharaoh Khufu, for whom the pyramid was built, must have changed his mind twice. Standard references indicate that originally, Khufu had planned a somewhat smaller pyramid with his burial chamber sunk deep into bedrock below the base. But as his aspirations grew, he twice enlarged the tomb's plan and each time ordered the burial chamber to be raised higher up in the pyramid. I didn't see how this premise that the design was improvised and constantly changing could account for the way the pyramid's dimensions miniaturize the dimensions of the world and symbolize the positions of the stars.

Nevertheless, scholars couldn't bring themselves to believe that there might have been some still-secret purpose in building the two vacant chambers into the pyramid. (Nor would they admit the possibility of some other recess, never yet found, in which an unknown apparatus could disrupt the cosmic rays that Dr. Alvarez tried to count.)

Anyhow, the King's Chamber—a big high-ceilinged room—was roofed with a series of six enormous granite slabs that formed five stress-relieving compartments. Critics nowadays claimed that the old Egyptian master builders misjudged their stresses and strains; that only one hollow space would have sufficed to reduce the downward pressure. I didn't think the pyramid builders were omniscient. But I might point out that we tend to forget, in our own day of electronically analyzed T-beams, that the architects of only a few decades ago used to build with a safety factor of five, eight, or even twelve.

When Khufu died and was embalmed, attendants presumably put his mummy into a wooden coffin. They bore the coffin up the Ascending Corridor, through the Grand Gallery, and into the King's Chamber. There they set the coffin into a plain granite sarcophagus, which must have been installed early in the construction of the pyramid, because it is a little too wide to go through the narrow passage to the King's Chamber. The sarcophagus had a heavy stone lid. When this lid slid into place, stone bolts were shoved into place across it, thus securing the lid—they apparently thought—for all time.

On their way out, the workmen carefully jerked loose a set of props in the vestibule of the King's Chamber. This allowed three huge portcullis blocks to crash to the floor, blocking the vestibule.

In the Grand Gallery, workmen eased stone blocks down into the Ascending Corridor. When they knocked out restraining crossbeams, these plugs slid down, sealing the corridor as well. Then the men in the gallery escaped down a shaft and up the Descending Corridor. These extraordinary measures foiled even the most ingenious tomb robbers for at least four centuries.

But there was still a puzzle, I thought. Because nothing was found inside when the Arab caliph's men smashed and battered their way to the King's Chamber, experts all assumed that thieves finally broke in and stole the mummy (why steal a mummy?) plus a great hoard of funerary treasures. On the other hand, if the Great Pyramid was never really intended for a tomb, nor ever used as one, then perhaps there were no thieves. In that case, precisely what was the purpose of building it and sealing it? I didn't know.

In the nineteenth century, when Darwin's theory of evolution set science on a collision course with established religion, speculation about the purpose of the Great Pyramid increased. Bible students thought they saw all sorts of significance in it. Believers in the occult pored over interior measurements and concluded that the austere unadorned Grand Gallery foretold the key dates in the history of man, if an arbitrary measurement called a "pyramid inch" were taken as the equal of a year.

The earliest group of these enthusiasts deduced from their count of pyramid inches that a great miracle, comparable to a second coming of Christ, would occur in 1881. When no miracle became noticeable in

1881, another group inched along the passages with tapes and transits and worked out another, more elaborate prophecy. They said a great war would break out in 1928 and Christ would come again in 1936.

After 1936, undiscouraged pyramid lovers reshuffled the numbers and amended their predictions. This time they said a world-shaking event was predestined for 1953. When that year also passed rather quietly, so many farfetched predictions had been based on so many dubious mathematical calculations that a kind of revulsion set in. The educated public turned from the subject in disgust, leaving it almost entirely to the Sunday supplements and the pulp magazines.

My own explorations of the pyramid shed no additional light, but did leave me more suspicious than ever that intelligent beings from outer space might have taken a hand in mankind's development from time to time. And I wondered more than ever whether someday there would be additional—and more startling—discoveries about the pyramids.

I knew there could be any number of clues in the thousands of hieroglyphs and cuneiform texts in our libraries and museums, still lying undeciphered because of the ingrained reluctance of academicians to look at, let alone analyze, the evidence of the strangely advanced knowledge used in the construction of the Great Pyramid at Giza.

I thought about the pyramids in so many other parts of the world. In Petrie's day the Egyptian pyramids were believed to be unique. But later diggers found that there were pyramids in the Orient, pyramids in the British Isles, pyramids in South America, pyramids in North America. Were they related?

In the 1920s a group of amateur anthropologists who came to be called Diffusionists put forth the idea that all civilization could be traced back to Egypt, whence it was carried to other lands. According to the anatomist Sir Grafton Elliot Smith, the leading Diffusionist, someone from Egypt went to Mesopotamia and built—or more likely taught the natives to build—ziggurats in imitation of Egyptian pyramids.

Someone else from Egypt, it was said, repeated the performance in Cambodia, and others in Central America, where they discovered the forgotten empires on which the Aztec and Mayan civilizations were later founded.

Well, maybe. But pyramids could have been invented independently in each place where they appeared. They seemed to have different uses in different civilizations. And their architecture was different.

For example, Assyrian ziggurats—temples shaped like mountains—were built up in receding terraces formed by a sloping ramp that spiraled around the four sides from base to summit. At the summit a temple room served both as a shrine and as an observatory. Every city in Sumer, and later in Babylonia, contained within its walls a ziggurat. The priests supposedly thought that the height of a ziggurat would bring them near enough to the gods to make their prayers more audible.

Great height did seem to be a common factor among pyramids of many lands. The highest building in the Americas, before the construction of New York's skyscrapers, was a deserted Mayan temple in Tikal, Guatemala, now simply designated as Tikal IV. It soared to a height of 212 feet. However, its steeply rising blocks made it more like a tower than an Egyptian pyramid. It also was topped by a ritual chamber, which apparently was never to be found at the top of any pyramid in Egypt.

I thought the ancient Toltec pyramids could be the most interesting of all New World pyramids. I delved further into the known facts about them.

In 1925 archaeologists digging out a pyramid at the northwest edge of modern Mexico City found that they were working not on one pyramid, but on eight—an onion in stone, as one writer called it—one shell nested within another. Other data indicated that a shell had probably been added every fifty-two years. So the arithmetic seemed to show that this pyramid alone had been worked on for more than four centuries. Except for the cathedral building of Europe, no single architectural project anywhere had ever continued so long.

Fifty miles south of Mexico City, diggers found remains of a Toltec pyramid that once covered a larger area than the Great Pyramid of Egypt. There were labyrinthine passages eleven hundred yards long.

The most controversial of the Toltec pyramids was unearthed at the southern fringe of Mexico City. It was controversial because a lava flood had evidently covered half of it at some time after it was completed. The archaeologists, hoping to get a clearer fix on the age of the pyramid, called on geologists for help.

"How old is this lava?" the archaeologists asked.

The geologists, not realizing that their answer was knocking the whole historical timetable out of focus, answered eight thousand years.

If the answer was right, it meant that the Toltec culture was a thousand years older than any yet uncovered in the Old World. Older than Sumer and Akkad, than Babylon, than Egypt. But maybe the geologists' answer was wrong. The controversy still rages.

At any rate, there did seem to be certain striking similarities between the Egyptian pyramids and those elsewhere. A lot of them had tunnels, mostly leading downward. One such passage (in a cone-shaped pyramid in the Orkney Islands) is fifty-four feet long, and aimed telescopically at a huge stone that indicates the summer solstice.

Another similarity was the staircase running up the center of many pyramids. Of course it's logical to include a staircase in almost any high-rise stone structure, because staircases are useful for climbing to the top. However, a staircase could also provide a fixed meridian slot for observing the stars.

What was it about pyramids, I wondered, that fascinated so many ancient peoples? Was it the resemblance to a mountain? Mountains had always attracted prophets. Was it the spatial complex—the outline that suggested a prospect of infinity? Or was it because they looked like stately stairways leading on and up into the inner reaches of heaven? Or was it because their peepholes in the masonry helped men study the movements of the faraway celestial bodies?

This much I knew: the Mayan, Aztec, and Toltec cultures were related. All three societies built pyramids with steps leading up to a flat summit. Their pyramids were all located according to astronomical lines of sight, and were correlated with a long-term calendar cycle.

Beyond that, the facts were inadequate. No panoramic picture of any grand diffusion from a central spore had yet emerged clearly, nor had anything come out that could demolish any of the various speculations about helpful beings from another planet. We could spin theories, but we might never know.

# XI

## *A Heretic at Karnak*

Thirty-three centuries ago, at Karnak on the east bank of the Nile, an extraordinary temple arose. It became the largest religious building in the world—and was never exceeded by any built later.

I went to see it because its story was interwoven with the story of a man who came 1,270 years after Imhotep, yet seemed almost as significant.

The massive temple complex was well worth seeing for itself. It proved—in a different way than the pyramids had proven in previous centuries—that the Egyptians were the greatest builders in history.

Karnak's Hypostyle Hall (from the Greek, meaning "resting on pillars") was the largest single chamber of any temple in the world. It covered fifty-four thousand square feet, almost equal to the space occupied by one of the greatest cathedrals of medieval Europe—Canterbury in England.

The hall's monolithic pillars stood like giant tree trunks in a forest. A number of them were thirty-three feet in girth—so wide that a dozen men could have been hidden by one—and were sixty-nine feet high. They were crowned by spreading capitals of such size that one hundred men could stand on one. The rest were forty-three feet high.

This hall with its 136 tremendous columns was only the central feature of a building complex that could cover much of mid-Manhattan. Within the walls there could be room for Saint Peter's in Rome, the Milan

Cathedral, and Notre Dame in Paris. Surrounding the temple were many courts, and avenues lined with sphinxes, obelisks, pylons, and statues. The outer walls could comfortably enclose ten European cathedrals.

This complex, the most massive of all time, stood intact for little more than two decades. Then the Egyptians themselves destroyed much of it. For years modern scholars have been slowly recreating it block by block, in response to one of Egyptology's most difficult challenges.

For me the challenge was different.

I wanted to try to fathom the life and works of the man who built part of Karnak—and who inaugurated a religious revolution that brought the whole structure of imperial Egypt down upon his head.

The man was known to history as Akhenaten or Ikhnaton. He was described by the great American Egyptologist James H. Breasted as "the world's first idealist . . . the earliest monotheist, and the first prophet of internationalism—the most remarkable figure of the Ancient World before the Hebrews."

Ikhnaton went down in Egypt's archives as the heretic pharaoh. Breaking with a thousand years of tradition and superstition, for a few brief years he ruled a kingdom of peace, love, and beauty. I wondered if he, like Imhotep and the legendary Thoth, might have been guided by an intelligence older than mankind.

The Egypt of Ikhnaton was vastly different from the Egypt of Imhotep and the pyramid builders. When he ascended the ancient throne of the pharaohs in 1380 B.C., probably at the age of fifteen, he found himself ruling an empire that stretched from Ethiopia to the Euphrates. Egypt's elegant simplicity of clothing had been superseded when the nation fattened on the tribute of Asia and the commerce of the Mediterranean world; jewelry and rich full robes became a passion with all classes. Every merchant had his seal of silver or gold. Every man had a ring, every woman an ornamental chain, some five feet in length. Men

and women and even teen-agers wore heavy earrings,
bracelets, pendants, and beads of costly stone.

The capital city, Thebes, was as majestic as any in
history. Her streets were thronged with merchants, her
markets filled with the goods of the world, her buildings "surpassing in magnificence all those of ancient
or modern capitals." Her massive temples groaned
with offerings. At Karnak the lordly Promenade and
Festival Hall rose to the greater glory of pharaoh and
the gods.

The priests were no longer deeply learned men.
Now they were just the necessary props of the throne,
and the secret police of the social order. In effect,
though not in law, the office of priest passed down
from father to son, so a class had grown up that became richer and stronger than the feudal aristocracy
or the royal family itself. The sacrifices offered to the
gods supplied the priests with food and drink. The
temple buildings gave them spacious homes. The rev-
enues of lands dedicated to the gods brought them
ample incomes.

This was Egypt in the days of her greatest grandeur, in the dynasty before her fall. The boy-emperor
felt she had gone astray.

His royal name was Amenhotep IV. It contained the
name of Amen because sacred tradition required that
every ruler should be a "son" of the great god Amen,
lord of Karnak and principal deity of all. The young
pharaoh's own great-grandfather Amenhotep II had
sacrificed six captive Syrian kings to Amen with his
own hand. The most beautiful girl among the noble
families of Thebes was always chosen to be conse-
crated to Amen (which probably meant in practice
that she was a captive to amuse the priests).

But this pharaoh wanted nothing to do with Amen,
whose name meant "the Hidden One." He was sick of
the corruption of the priesthood. He set out to abolish
the worship of Amen and of the other gods and goddesses of Egypt. He ordered the closing of their
shrines—the shrines to Heqet the frog goddess, to
Wadjit the cobra goddess, to Nekhbet the vulture
goddess, to Tqurt the pregnant hippopotamus who

watched over childbirth. Down with the monkey god, the jackal god, the moon god, the plant gods, the wind gods, the human gods, and countless lesser divinities!

In their place, he said, would be only one god, Aton—whose symbol he ordered carved in limestone friezes: a disk with rays that stretched downward to the ground, ending in small hands.

According to legend, he said this disk represented the Sun. Translators gave this meaning to every Egyptian writing about it. But as I looked at the carved disk with hands attached to beams, I couldn't help wondering whether it had a double meaning. Could it symbolize a disk-shaped spacecraft, inhabited by beings with helping hands, radiating energy?

I felt sure the Egyptians wondered about Aton too, for different reasons. Why did they need Aton as a sun god? They already had Amen, who the priests said was god of the Sun. They also had Re or Ra, whose center was at Heliopolis, and who was a sun god too; sometimes both gods combined into one as Amen-Re. If this iconoclastic pharaoh wished everyone to worship the Sun, why did they need a new god for that?

Such mutterings probably never reached his ears. He went happily ahead trying to suppress all the old sects. In the sixth year of his reign he shocked Egypt by changing his name to Ikhnaton—meaning "He who serves Aton" or "Aton is satisfied." His mind was full of new ideas—and his ideas would be seen by subsequent cultures as original contributions to man's understanding of the world. Even his preaching that the Sun was a source of life and energy was a religious expression of what would eventually be known as a scientific fact.

He composed a hymn to Aton, the greatest poetry that survived from ancient Egypt. As I read it, many of its ambiguous lines hinted again that perhaps he knew something about spacecraft, panspermia, and the peculiar creative powers attributed to the god at Tiahuanaco:

O living Aton, beginning of life,
Creator of the germ in woman,
Maker of seed in man,
Giver of breath to animate every one that he maketh!

How manifold are thy works!
They are hidden from before us,
O sole god, whose powers no other possesseth. . . .

All that are on high,
That fly with their wings,
Thou suppliest their necessities. . . .

How excellent are thy designs,
O Lord of eternity!
There is a Nile in the sky for the strangers
And for the cattle of every country. . . .

Dawning, glittering, going afar and returning,
Thou makest millions of forms
Through thyself alone. . . .

You created the strange countries as well as the land
    of Egypt,
You set every man in his place.
Men speak in many tongues, in body and complexion
    they are various,
For you have distinguished between people and peo-
    ple. . . .

There is no other that knoweth thee
Save thy son Ikhnaton.
Thou hast made him wise
In thy plans and in thy strength. . . .

As far as anyone knows today, this was mankind's
first outstanding expression of monotheism—seven
hundred years before Isaiah. It is strongly echoed, of
course, in the 104th Psalm. How the words came down
to the Hebrew psalmist no one can say.

As Akbar would in India thirty centuries later,
Ikhnaton seemed to see divinity in the Sun as the
source of all earthly light and life. He also saw mankind as one brotherhood. He conceived his god as be-
longing to all nations equally, and even named other
countries before his own as being in the care of Aton.

What an astounding advance on the old sectarian vengeful gods!

If Ikhnaton was indeed being advised by visitors from another world, they evidently knew less about human nature than they did about arts and sciences. It was one of the tragedies of history that Ikhnaton, having caught his vision of universal unity, was not satisfied to let the nobility of his new religion slowly win the hearts of men.

With a poet's audacity he threw compromise to the wind, and tried to impose Aton on his people by law. Vulgar idolatry must cease, he proclaimed. The new god was never to be portrayed in human or animal form (was there someone with him he didn't want identified?) and never to be bribed with spells and charms.

To enforce this monotheism, Ikhnaton declared all creeds but his own illegal, and commanded once more that all the old temples should be closed. As a substitute he built at Karnak the great open-court temple to Aton—surrounded by twenty-seven more-than-life-size statues of himself. I was amazed that such a devout man could be so in love with his own image. But perhaps, I thought, he believed that his people's loyalty to their pharaohs would help establish the new religion, because the statues emphasized his endorsement of it.

This was a mistake. And he made a worse mistake. He finally gave orders that the names of all gods but Aton should be effaced and chiseled from every public inscription in Egypt. He even mutilated his father's name on a hundred monuments by cutting out the word *Amen.*

When he defaced his father's name, it seemed to his subjects a blasphemous impiety. Few things were more important to them than honoring the ancestral dead. He overestimated the capacity of the people to rise above superstition.

And he underestimated the power and tenacity of the priesthood. For the past thousand years, at least, priests had been enlarging their wealth and influence. As early as the Fifth Dynasty, pharaohs excused priests from lending servants for public works, and later exempted priests from turning over to the national coffers a share of the yield of their lands. These concessions hurt the national economy, for they kept from the treasury riches that the government might have used for the welfare of the people. A time was coming when the treasury would not have enough income to keep the people fed.

Exemption from taxes was only the start of the priests' enrichment. With Egypt's foreign conquests, they grew richer still on booty, as the gods were paid tribute for every military victory. By Ikhnaton's time the priests were the richest and most influential men in Egypt, and ruled almost in partnership with the pharaoh.

Most powerful of all were the priests of Amen of Thebes. The high priest of Amen controlled one of the greatest landholdings of the ancient world; some estimates put it as high as 30 percent of all land in Egypt.

The priesthood was also entrenched in its power over the populace. A million proud citizens of Egypt believed that their many gods, propitiated by the priests, had shown favor in enabling the nation to expand into an empire. So the common man willingly gave the gods an active hand in his daily affairs. Priests were busy selling charms, mumbling incantations, and performing magic rites for pay. At every step the pious Egyptian had to utter strange formulas to shield himself from evil and attract good luck. Every door needed a god or two to frighten away malign spirits and ensure a safe passage into the hereafter.

As Breasted wrote in *Ancient Times: A History of the Early World*, "Thus the earliest moral development which we can trace in the ancient East was suddenly arrested, or at least checked, by the detestable devices of a corrupt priesthood eager for gain."

Obviously Ikhnaton was trying to bring about social reforms in the guise of a religious reformation. Did a revelation inspire him, as in the case of other prophets? Or was his new doctrine an intellectual feat all his own?

He and his beautiful young Queen Nefertiti, who enthusiastically shared her husband's faith, abandoned the capital city Thebes as sinful, and sailed down the Nile to found their City of God. Almost halfway to Memphis they came to a place on the eastern side where the cliffs curved away from the river to enclose a crescent of desert land. Nothing was there but a few peasants' houses along the fertile bank.

Ikhnaton spent the night in the royal tent, then mounted his golden chariot and rode across the plain until the Sun's rays shining on him told him to stop. There he fixed the southern boundary of his new city, midway between Egypt's northern and southern frontiers, on virgin soil never before dedicated to any god.

He made offerings to Aton, then issued a proclamation to his followers. Rather touchingly he said that no human being had advised him to come here. "No, it was the Aton himself who urged me to build this city," he declared. He named the new capital Akhetaton, "City of the Horizon of Aton."

A beautiful new city arose with surprising speed. In two years it was complete with palaces and public buildings, and ready for occupants. The transporting of the king and his loyal subjects to the new city was a tremendous undertaking. Hundreds of boats sailed down the Nile, laden with families and all their possessions.

Water and soil had been brought to Akhetaton. It was green with gardens and parks, laid out informally instead of in the conventional grids of Thebes. For the next few years, life in the Horizon City was probably happier than in any other city since.

Its doctrine proclaimed that the new god "lived on truth." Truth became the watchword of the joyous religion. For the heretic pharaoh it not only meant truth in the conventional sense but an openness and an avoidance of hypocrisy, a determination to show things as they were. This affected not only the everyday life of the city but the style and content of its art works.

Artists were much honored at Akhetaton, and their houses and studios were in the best streets. Some of the finest examples of all Egyptian art were created there. Taking their cue from the pharaoh's concept of a nature-loving deity, artists represented every form of plant and animal life with startling realism and a perfection hardly surpassed in any other place or time.

Ikhnaton and Nefertiti set an example of natural family life. They kissed and embraced their children in public, and took them driving through the streets and let them hold the horses' reins. More daringly, they refused to let artists portray them in the stiff idealized way that all pharaohs had previously been shown. They insisted on realism. The frozen dignity of imperial Egypt was false, they said.

Taking Ikhnaton at his word, the artists probably exaggerated his physical oddities. They made paintings and sculptures showing him as a youth of gentle thin face, with large eyelids like a dreamer's, a long misshapen skull, drooping shoulders, fat belly, and spindly legs—probably the outward signs of a glandular disorder. They also portrayed him in lively informal scenes, holding his wife on his knee or fondling his baby daughters.

Architects built temples open to the full sunshine, unlike the dark frightening sanctuaries of "the Hidden One." There was plenty of wealth, for nothing was spent on wars, and property owners paid the taxes that supported Aton's temples. The city grew lovelier every year as trees and gardens matured. Zoological gardens, pools, loggias, and sunken courts were open for the pleasure of residents. Breweries, bakeries, and stables added to the luxury. Long afterward, excavators even found a model village of small neat homes for the workmen employed in building the city.

There seemed to be just one minor mystery at Akhetaton. When artists pleaded with the pharaoh to describe his god so they could portray him, Ikhnaton was evasive. He said loftily that Aton had no form, and therefore could not be realistically shown. The symbol of the Sun disk would have to do.

He was absorbed in transforming Egypt internally, hardly glancing at reports from the provinces. He was locked in a struggle with the priesthood and the bureaucracy. For his own administrative organization he drew heavily on the army and on "new men," promoted from humble origins. The fact that those of noble birth seemed to try to play down their lineage was proof that a genuine element of social revolution was at work. There were indications, too, that the Horizon City gave more freedom and a higher status to women.

But trouble was brewing. The pharaoh's idealism and pacifism made him neglect the empire and its enemies. When monarchs with whom he was allied in Syria and Palestine appealed for military help, he hesitated. He was not sure that Egypt should be entangled in alliances, or keep other peoples subjugated. And he was loath to send Egyptians to die on distant fields.

So he sent no troops. In 1893 Sir William Petrie, digging in the dead ruins of the city, found more than 350 cuneiform letter-tablets, of which most were appeals for aid addressed to Ikhnaton by the governors of his provinces or by the heads of allied nations.

When the dependencies saw that they were dealing with a saint, they deposed their Egyptian governors, quietly stopped all payment of tribute, and became virtually free nations again.

Meanwhile, behind the scenes in Thebes and Heliopolis, the priests plotted and prepared. In the seclusion of their own homes the populace continued to worship their innumerable ancient fearsome gods. A hundred crafts whose livelihoods depended on the decaying temples muttered in secret against the heretic. Even in his palace at Akhetaton his ministers and generals apparently despised him and prayed for his death, for was he not allowing the empire to fall apart in his hands?

Everything began to go badly for the pharaoh and

those who loved him. The second daughter of Nefertiti and Ikhnaton, the princess Meketaton, died. The disk god had not, after all, granted her long life. The pharaoh had six daughters but no son; and though by law he might have sought a male heir by a secondary wife, he would not, but remained faithful to Nefertiti. His treasury had long depended on foreign tribute—and suddenly it was almost empty. Domestic taxes were minimal, and the working of the gold mines had stopped. Every colony was in revolt and every power in Egypt was arrayed against him, waiting for his fall.

At this point Ikhnaton and Nefertiti disappeared from the records.

Like figures in some glorious dream, they faded out of history. Archaeologists could discover no mention of how or where they died; a tomb prepared for them in the cliffs near Akhetaton was found, but it was empty. What a strange coincidence, I thought, that the two greatest innovators in Egyptian history—Imhotep and Ikhnaton—both vanished without a trace!

The nineteen-year reign of Ikhnaton puzzled all historians. Leonard Cottrell wrote, "It was one of the most curious episodes in the history of the ancient world, and we do not yet completely understand its cause or its effects. It arose from the personality of one individual. ... Around the figure of this king controversy has raged. Was he genius or madman?"

In Arnold Toynbee's monumental *Study of History*, this great authority passes his own judgment: "The best proof that the restored Egyptiac society was void of life was the complete failure of the one attempt to raise it from the dead. ... By sheer genius Ikhnaton created a new conception of God and man, life and nature, and expressed it in a new art and poetry; but dead societies cannot thus be brought to life. His failure is the proof that we are justified in regarding the social phenomena of Egyptiac history from the sixteenth century B.C. onwards as an epilogue rather than as the history of a new society."

Soon after Ikhnaton ceased to be heard of, the priests of Amen took control again. The young pharaoh Tutankhamen, who had been born into the Aton faith as Tutankhaton, changed his name and, while still a child, returned to Thebes, where he announced to a rejoicing people the restoration of the ancient gods and the renewal of all the feast days that had been abolished.

The chisel wielders reappeared to hack out Ikhnaton's name from all monuments and to recarve the names he had removed. The priests forbade the name of the revolutionary pharaoh or his capital city to pass any man's lips, and the people referred to him only as the "Great Criminal."

The beautiful city of Akhetaton was abandoned, and fell into ruins that slept undisturbed until the arrival of nineteenth-century Egyptologists. At Karnak the temple to Aton was razed to the ground, and its stones were cannibalized for new and more colossal monuments to later pharaohs and their gods.

In a proclamation inscribed on the walls at Karnak, Tutankhamen reported that all the way from Elephantine to the delta, the temples and shrines of the gods and goddesses had "fallen into desolation and become ruins overgrown with weeds, their chapels as though they had never been. . . . The land was upside down, and the gods turned their backs on it."

For the rest Tutankhamen reigned without distinction. He died at eighteen and left no son to succeed him. The world would hardly have heard of him had not fabulous treasures been found in his grave. After him a doughty general, Harmhab, became pharaoh. He marched his armies up and down the coast to win back, temporarily, much of the territory lost under Ikhnaton.

Having been Ikhnaton's army commander, Harmhab must have at least pretended to worship Aton. Later, as ruler of Egypt, he was probably embarrassed about his background of heresy. To distract attention from it, he staged a great show of vandalism at Karnak. Under his direction workmen defaced every image of Nefertiti they could find on the segments of pillars from her dismantled courtyard. They also scratched out the sunray hands of Aton wherever these were shown. Then they turned the blocks upside down and

concealed them inside huge new pillars being erected. Thus the former commoner Harmhab demonstrated his contempt for the discarded royal family,
and supposedly put the queen out of men's sight forever. Not until 1965, when archaeologists began
studying the rubble of Karnak, did the mutilated
blocks come to light.

Pharaohs of the nineteenth dynasty succeeded
Harmhab, and commemorated their exploits by enlarging the colossal stoneworks at Karnak. Architecture was self-consciously swelling with a kind of
Ozymandian symbolism, and painting and sculpture
were becoming cruder, as part of the violent reaction
against Ikhnaton's tragic attempt at reform.

According to Spengler's concept of historical cycles,
the grandiose structures of Egypt's last imperial chapter were a close parallel to the enormous buildings
and statues created during the decadent era of imperial Rome. Other examples of the "colossal" historical
phase were the period when Sennacherib built up
Nineveh, when Emperor Huang-ti ruled in China, and
when the enormous Hindu monuments were erected
in India after A.D. 1250. We saw something similar in
the vast ornate structures put up in America from the
1890s through the 1920s, and again in Hitler's Berlin.

Buildings mirror the life of the individual and the
race. The shell that human beings create for themselves marks their inner nature as plainly as that of a
snail denotes its species. Karnak reflects the whole
tragic story of Egypt's final burst of giantism.

Where Imhotep had succeeded, Ikhnaton failed. He
was millennia ahead of his time. Nevertheless the
winds and sands destroyed only the body of ancient
Egypt. Its spirit lived on in the folkways and achievements of our race.

We who feel so little spiritual relation to the ancient Egyptian still use his things, as we sit on a four-
legged chair at a four-legged table, writing with a
pen on a piece of paper. We inherited Egypt's inventions of glass and linen, of the calendar and the clock,
of geometry and the alphabet. We inherited its advancement of medicine, of primary and secondary

education, even of technical training for office and administration. We benefited from the first clear formulation known to us of individual and public conscience, the first cry for social justice, the first widespread monogamy, the first monotheism, the first essays in moral philosophy. Through the Phoenicians, the Syrians, and the Jews, through the Cretans, the Greeks, and the Romans, the civilization of Egypt passed down to become part of mankind's heritage. What Egypt accomplished at the very dawn of history gave impetus to many nations who followed her.

With the end of my prowlings in Egypt, I had traveled back as far as I could down the dim corridors of time—as an eyewitness, at least. What I had learned in my wanderings fortified parts of my outlandish premise. In the rise and decline of the Egyptian empire, I found support for the possibility that sudden setbacks wipe out centuries of achievement. I was more confident that the generating force of Sumer and Egypt could have been products of the leftover gleanings of predestruction colonists. It was possible that substantive ideas took root in the stabilized environment of the Nile Delta, and became the basis for the advancement of mankind. I had a clearer image of a distant past where man had small, widely separated footholds in a vast unpopulated sphere. At the centers of these encampments were people who returned information from a richer past and utilized it to meet the demands of their immediate present. I think I knew better why tales of Atlantis ring so true. There was an Atlantis, probably dozens of them, owing their origin to the Tiahuanaco wellspring. At least that was my surmise. There were more details to be found in China and Tibet. For the moment they were off limits to me. And so I knew of no other ancient places on earth where on-the-spot investigation might show me any additional faint clues to the presence of departed visitors from outside our universe.

However, there were still certain knowledgeable people who might give me further evidence in face-to-face conversation. I would go and talk with them.

# XII

## Back to the Bible

"I began with a completely negative viewpoint," Joseph Blumrich told me. "Ideas about the earth being visited long ago by spacemen were completely untenable, in my opinion." He had just completed a book called *The Spaceships of Ezekiel*, and I wanted to know the basis for his work.

"You were negative because of your engineering background?" I was interviewing him at Huntsville, Alabama, where he works for the National Aeronautics and Space Administration (NASA).

"Well, yes. I started in aircraft engineering in 1934. I've worked in aerospace engineering since 1959. And as an engineer, I just laughed when someone said that spacecraft were described by the prophet Ezekiel."

"But you changed your mind?"

He nodded. "To refute him, I looked up the Book of Ezekiel. Right in the first chapter—it was verse seven—I found a sentence that was meaningless to Biblical scholars and nontechnical people, but as a spacecraft designer I happened to understand exactly what it meant."

He handed me a Bible, and I opened it to reread Ezekiel's story of his "vision." Generations of theologists have classified this story as symbolic fantasy. They were baffled to explain what it symbolized.

The young Hebrew prophet Ezekiel, I remembered, belonged to a priestly family that had been driven to

Babylon in the first deportation from Jerusalem. He had been in exile for five years (some time during the sixth century before Christ) when he beheld what he allegedly said were visions of God.

The first vision had come, according to the Book of Ezekiel, by the river Chebar. On the green banks of that alien stream, he looked up and saw something coming in on a great wind from the north.

"Have you ever noticed?" I asked Blumrich. "Just as in the Bible, there were tales in ancient Egypt and China of airborne visitors dropping in from the north. Today there's a theory that if starships came to Earth, the safest route for an approach might be from the direction of Polaris, the north star, in order to take advantage of the polar gaps in the Van Allen radiation belt. . . . Well, back to Ezekiel."

The Bible's description of Ezekiel's vision was that he saw a great cloud, with fire flashing through it, and a radiance around it. Something gleamed like metal in the midst of it. He heard "the noise of great waters." From the cloud descended what resembled four animals.

I said, "Having looked at pictures of lunar landing craft descending slowly in a fiery cloud created by their downdraft, seeming to stand on a tail of jet exhaust, I can conceive that the ancients might have described them somewhat as Ezekiel did. Of course we don't know exactly what he said. His translators from the Aramaic had no idea what he was talking about—"

"Right. Let's move on to verse seven," Blumrich said. "That was a key section."

The sentence read, *"They had straight legs and hoofs like calves, glittering like polished brass."*

"At other places Ezekiel refers to them as round feet," Blumrich said. "This description sounded strikingly like an aerospace structure I happened to know about, because I'd been closely involved with it."

"A structure for a soft landing, you mean?"

He nodded. "From 1962 to 1964 I was chief of a group in NASA that had the assignment of figuring out the design options for landing gear of a hypo-

thetical unmanned lunar landing craft. Actually the
vehicle was never built, but finding the necessary
structure solutions was an important exercise. We
developed a landing gear with straight legs and what
we called footpads—things that might well have reminded Ezekiel of the round flat hoofs of an ox."

"This was one of many possible designs?" I asked.

"I don't think so. It turned out to be the most logical one we could imagine, after examining all the possibilities. And it worked well. After designing it, we
built those round footpads and road-tested them,
pulling them over various materials to find their sliding behavior. We became convinced that anyone
who wanted to land a vehicle gently on a hard surface, and move around on it safely, would find that
our footpads could do the job best. Consequently
when I read Ezekiel it came to my mind immediately
that this could be a direct technical description."

"That's interesting as far as it goes," I pressed, "but
what about Ezekiel's description of the vehicle as a
whole?"

"You notice that he says these four figures descending through the cloud each had four wings. First he
calls the figures men. Then he switches, and for the
rest of the chapter he uses phrases like 'living creatures' and 'like men yet unlike them.' My wife and I
got all the Bibles in the house, German and English,
and compared the translations. It was a fascinating
night."

"Did you reach any conclusion about what these
four-winged creatures might be?"

"Of course. Helicopters. The wings were moving ro-
tor blades."

I leaned back and pondered. "A Hebrew prophet
wouldn't have any knowledge of helicopters and
rocket engines. So he could only describe what they
looked and sounded like, in his own familiar terms.
And he would probably think they were living giants,
because of all their noise and motion. . . . But I wonder why there should be four of them flying in formation."

"This was the clincher, to me," Blumrich said with

a smile. "I don't think they literally flew in formation, and Ezekiel doesn't say so. He says they were linked one to another."

"Would that be technically possible?" I asked.

"At first I thought it sounded crazy. But by this time I was taking Ezekiel seriously from an engineer's viewpoint. Remember, the man gave detailed descriptions of four encounters with spaceships. He said he actually flew with one, in chapter 8 of the Book of Ezekiel. It 'lifted him up between Earth and heaven,' and apparently landed him near the north gate of Jerusalem, where he used to live. He explored the depravity of the city for a few days, then flew back to the Chebar. Ezekiel seemed to have an enormous memory and an excellent ability to observe and describe. So I kept fiddling around with his descriptions, trying to figure how the four helicoptors could be tied together. What was the center body of the structure? I tried several solutions and didn't get to a good end."

I smiled. "Sounds like you're leading up to something. Eventually you figured out what Ezekiel might have seen?"

"It was more like remembering than figuring out. All of a sudden it occurred to me that several years ago I had read in an engineering magazine a paper in which Roger Anderson described a high-drag aerodynamic body that would travel through the vacuum of outer space, then drop down for a soft landing through a planetary atmosphere such as Earth's."

I raised an eyebrow. "Why did he design such a body? Our space program didn't need anything like that, did it?"

"Not then. And not now. We've always used a reentry system where a space capsule drops like a stone, shedding its heat shield as it comes, then deploys parachutes for a splashdown in the open sea. But someday we'll need shuttle ships that fly from an orbiting mother ship to Earth and back again. Engineers like to noodle plans that will be needed several decades from now."

"You mean that such a shuttle ship may turn out to

be four copters fastened together into a single structure?" I demanded.

He grinned. "Strange as it seems, that's right. I
looked up Anderson's old article in a journal of the
American Institute of Aeronautics and Astronautics.
He had found that a configuration of four linked helicopters was an extremely useful aerodynamic body—
not only for space-Earth flight but for a variety of
other purposes. After he designed it, the NASA research center at Langley Field actually built a model
and tested it in wind tunnels, from subsonic to very
high hypersonic velocities. It proved out well. And
like any helicopter it was highly maneuverable, and
could hover at zero ground speed."

He showed me a sketch he had made. "Here's the total configuration. See the four helicopter units? This is
on a square arrangement, so two are here and one is
in front and one is behind. Now here's the center
body that carries these helicopters and ties them together. In coming down it was important, of course,
to provide a clean aerodynamic shape to achieve the
full effect of this quasi-conical body. For that purpose
there's no problem to swing the helicopters around
and arrange them that way. This clears the shape of
the drag body so that it becomes fully effective aero-
dynamically."

I studied the drawing.

Its center body was a pod similar to the lunar-land-
ing module of the Apollo spacecraft. "Is this Anderson's design? Or yours?"

"There's little if anything by me in what you see.
The critical influence was, as I said, Anderson's development, which consists of this configuration.
There's only this upper curve, which I suppose you
might call my invention. It gives it an aerodynamic
body that could ascend back into orbit. So I think
what you're looking at is just about what Ezekiel saw
and described in the Bible."

"The ship he saw was dependent on a mother ship
in orbit?"

"Oh, it had to be. A lash-up of four choppers and a

central body wouldn't be the kind of craft you'd use for long voyages in deep space."

I glanced back at the Bible. "There's still a problem: Ezekiel's strange description of the wheels. See what it says in verses fifteen through twenty-one? *'I looked at the animals; there was a wheel on the ground by each of them, one by each of the four. The wheels glittered like topaz. The four of them had the same shape and seemed to be made one inside another. They went forward four ways and kept their course unswervingly.'*"

"All interpreters of that passage missed the point," he said. "The solution is surprisingly simple once you know it."

He took a pencil and sketched rapidly. "Assume that you have the inner tube of a tire, which can roll in its plane as usual. If you twist the tire, now it rolls perpendicular to itself, to its main plane. The rest is just a conversion of that idea into engineering terms. I've come up with two possible solutions—you see one here—and I don't think there's any need for more, at least to show the feasibility. The wheel is the hub and spokes. The wheel obviously can roll as it is, forward or backward. Now if we drive a barrel-shaped section about its own axis, the wheel can roll out of the plane or into the plane—see? A combination of this drive and that rotation allows such a wheel to go in any direction. It may be of interest that I've filed for a patent on this. My filing was accepted and the patent is now being processed by the United States Patent Office."

I chuckled. "That's really one for the book. You've patented an invention described in the Old Testament."

"My patent," he said with a technical man's precision, "is based on my interpretation of the function of the wheel described by Ezekiel."

I read a few lines further in the Book of Ezekiel. "But look here. Ezekiel has more to say about these odd chariot wheels: *'As I looked at the wheels, lo! the rims of the four of them were full of eyes round about.'* What do you suppose that meant?"

"Ezekiel mentions several times that the rims of the wheels are covered with eyes—which of course is a very strange statement. Here's the wheel I sketched. If these barrel-shaped drums had a smooth surface they would slide. So it would be difficult to tightly control the vehicle's motion on the ground. The logical solution is to make short protrusions from the wheel surface. They bear into the ground as the wheel turns. They're almost like spikes, only stumpier. Have you ever seen the heavy road-building equipment called sheep's-foot rollers?"

I nodded. "As I recall, they're like steamrollers studded with short round cleats all over the roller."

"Sure. What Ezekiel called eyes are stubs that protrude from the surface of this bell-shaped roller, like bug eyes. They stick into the ground and prevent the vehicle from sliding."

"The prophet really did notice a lot of details, didn't he? Not many people could do as well in describing a complicated spacecraft without using technical terms. But wait a minute! I see we skipped right over something in Ezekiel's first chapter—the faces. He says the four creatures who came down out of a cloud had the faces of a man, a lion, an ox, and an eagle. Does that mean anything to an engineer?"

Blumrich shrugged. "Many machines have facelike structures. Everyone has seen faces in rocks, in clouds, in tree stumps. If you remember, our two-man Gemini spacecraft looked like a face from various angles. And the lunar lander had such a striking resemblance to a giant insect that we all called it the Bug."

"You think that the helicopters looked like different animal heads to Ezekiel?"

"Could be. He'd never seen a machine in his life, remember. With their noise and their motion, helicopters would seem to him to be living creatures. Now, in a normal helicopter as we build them today, the drive—the energy input—comes from below. So just below the plane of the rotors are gears and lever arms, and rods and so on, which stick out. These things may need some hood to protect them against dust or weather. So there often are sheet metal sec-

BACK TO THE BIBLE 141

tions with cutouts or humps to accommodate levers or rods. Some of them do have the distinct appearance of faces—topped by the whirling wings just as Ezekiel said."

I read on. *"Over the heads of the creatures was the semblance of a firmament, glittering like transparent ice, arched above their heads."* This certainly sounded as if it could be the transparent bubble in which helicopter pilots and passengers sit. *"And when they went, I heard the noise of their wings as they moved. It was like the sound of mighty waters. And when they stood still they let down their wings."*

I asked Blumrich, "Ezekiel says in this translation that above the four creatures he saw something *'shaped like a throne, with a semblance like that of a man sitting on it.'* And apparently he thought the being was God or the Lord, Yahweh. Who do you think it was?"

"He describes what would be called the command module in our space vehicles—and in that capsule is someone or something that he says looked like a man. In the original text he uses the word Adam to describe that man. He wouldn't have chosen this name to describe any supreme being. 'Adam' sounds more like the name he'd use for a prototype. I think he was conveying the information that he really saw something that looked like ourselves yet wasn't quite like us."

"Well, whoever it was gave him wise advice, apparently," I said. "Because from then on Ezekiel began to teach his fellow captives in exile the concept of individual responsibility. Sin wasn't communal, as the older notion had it. Repentance and salvation must also be individual. Each person would be rewarded or punished for his own deeds, not for those of his father or the tribe."

Blumrich agreed. "For the next twenty-three years or so Ezekiel was the real pastor of the exiled flock. If counselors from a star really paid him those four visits he described, they couldn't have singled out a better man as a conduit for advice. They must have had very good information about individual people, or else they just picked him at random. I've often wondered about that."

I wondered too, as I rode home from Huntsville.

I remembered other strange Bible stories. There was Exodus's mighty words about "thunders and lightnings, and a thick cloud upon the mount ... and Mount Sinai was altogether on a smoke, because the Lord descended upon it in fire." There was the good man Enoch who "walked with God" and was taken up by a "whirlwind" without having to die. There was Jonah, whose incredible sojourn in the belly of a whale might have been a trip in a submarine. There was the prophet Elijah, who heard a voice on Mount Horeb and departed from this earth riding in a "chariot of fire" which was "wrapped in a whirlwind."

There was Daniel's wondrous vision by a river of a being with "body flashing like the topaz, face like lightning, and eyes like lamps of fire." There were the various angels who came out of the sky and paid visits to Abraham, to Gideon, to Jacob, to Joshua, and to Lot. And there were the psalmists directing man's gaze to the depths beyond the stars.

What of all the similar myths and legends that went back much earlier than the Bible?

What of the flying carpets and giant birds in so many eastern wonder tales? What of Ayar Cachi, the flying Inca who allegedly had been "coming in the air with great wings" and landed in the Cuzco Valley?

What of the Greek myth of the fabulously skilled inventor and technician Daedalus, who sailed through the sky from Crete to Sicily, and of his son Icarus, who flew too close to the sun and fell to his death in the sea?

Virgil wrote of this legend. So did Ovid, Plutarch, and Diodorus Siculus and before them the Greek poets Epimenides, Bacchylides, Cleidemus, and Philochorus. Homer sang of Daedalus in the *Iliad*. Not until the excavations in 1881 by archaeologist Heinrich Schliemann did the world learn to its astonishment that some Greek legends had to be taken seriously after all. And not until Arthur Evans spent a quarter-century digging up the palace of King Minos at Knossos, with its legendary maze, did the world begin to believe that the maze-maker Daedalus might have been a real person. How many of the myths of flight might someday turn out to be based on the other-worldly technology described in the Book of Ezekiel?

I remembered that I'd heard eerie echoes of the same theme in Egypt. Its ancient Book of the Dead made several mentions of "the Shining Ones who live in rays of light," and contained other intriguing phrases such as "I course through space and time." It repeatedly referred to "winged disks" and "legions in the sky."

Everywhere I'd been, everywhere I'd delved into old cultures, the theme of flight kept reappearing. Interwoven with this theme were one or two subthemes that some of America's astronauts had found interesting. I decided to chat with Scott Carpenter about a view of Earth that few modern men had been privileged to see firsthand.

# XIII

## *Looking down on Earth*

One of the most fascinating puzzles in the history of geography is this: How much did ancient people know about the world before they had any apparent way of finding out?

Now that we have at last explored and mapped the seas and islands and continents, we're beginning to realize that the pitiable folks of antiquity, who we thought were sadly lacking in information about distant lands, were perhaps not as totally ignorant as we have always assumed.

In some mysterious way, all sorts of queer details about faraway places that still remained officially undiscovered had nevertheless found their way into the waterfront taverns of every European harbor. As early as the era of the Roman Empire, there was talk that somewhere far to the East, beyond India, lived a powerful people to whom the Greeks had given the name Seres—but just where the land of the Seres was, and what kind of people they were, nobody knew. Nobody in the West had seen a Chinese. Nor had anyone in China seen a European—although there were fables in China of cultivated nations far beyond the Asian steppes.

Then too, there was the perennial legend of a vast continent at the other side of the Atlantic. Five hundred years before Christ, such talk not only circulated but was written down to puzzle countless later generations of cartographers. The classical Romans mentioned this continent as an actual fact, and even knew the name. It was called Ultima Thule. By about A.D. 150 the Greek traveler and geographer Pausanias was writing that far west of the ocean there lay a group of islands whose inhabitants were red skinned and whose hair was black and coarse like that of a horse. Unless we assume that the skin and the hair were figments of Pausanias's imagination, we can't explain his report otherwise than as describing American Indians.

Where did such reports come from? Did they find their way to Europe from Vinland by way of Greenland and Iceland and the Faroe Islands? Or was it carried to Europe by those French fishermen who seemed to have known about the Banks of Newfoundland centuries before Columbus was born? Or was there another, stranger source of information?

In medieval Europe, curious odds and ends of fact and fancy grew into a vast conglomeration of seaman's folklore. This nautical mythology was full of foolishness and tall tales, yet it contained nuggets of truth that we can't wave away as the silly talk of a skipper in his cups.

For example, there were those recurring tales about Prester John, the mysterious priest-king who ruled a Christian country in the heart of Africa or somewhere. For a long time all intelligent geographers scoffed at this story. Then the rediscovery of Ethiopia by the Portuguese revealed that such a dark-skinned African potentate, who was also the head of a Christian church dating back at least nine centuries, really existed.

And there were the widespread rumors of a freakish people in the polar regions who had no necks, whose faces were on their chests, and whose feet were large enough to shade themselves from the sun. The credulous medieval populace believed these tales, but educated people certainly didn't—until the exploration of Greenland in the sixteenth century, when the fabled monsters turned out to be the furclad snowshoed Eskimo of Baffin Bay. With this discovery, antiquarians suddenly remembered Plato's discredited dialogue about a land where people lived in almost unbroken sunshine for as long as thirty days at a time, during which the sun went below the horizon for only about an hour each night. How could Plato or his contemporaries have known about the undiscovered Arctic Circle?

As for Antarctica, there was strange-sounding talk about it too, long before it was explored. As late as the start of this century some geographers still believed that the land sighted here and there beyond the storms and pack ice of the Southern Ocean might be merely a series of islands. Inasmuch as the Arctic was an ocean, covered with drifting masses of ice, the processes of nature would doubtless create the same sort of ocean at the opposite pole. Yet sailors claimed it was an enormous expanse of land. How could they possibly have a clue? No place in the world was as cold as the South Polar Plateau; there wasn't a single tree or settlement within two thousand miles of the pole. Only two parties of explorers had ever gone near it.

And yet the sailors' stories again proved right. We know now that Antarctica is a continent almost as large as Europe and Australia combined. Even now, however, a thousand-mile stretch of its coastline has never been reached by any ship, and man has set foot on less than 1 percent of its area.

In the time of Christ, people had heard of the bits of land now known as Madeira and the Cape Verde Islands and the Canary Islands and the Azores. But geographers kept insisting for more than a thousand years that there were no such island groups way out toward the west, where rumor placed them. Still, the word-of-mouth accounts were too full of concrete details to have been entirely invented. Somebody in ancient times had actually seen all those islands.

The most stubborn myth in the history of exploration was Australia. The Renaissance inherited from antiquity the notion that there existed a great unknown southern continent, usually designated on maps as Terra Australis Incognita, although a map drawn by Pomponius Mela in A.D. 40 (and still preserved today) called it the Antipodes. Century af-

ter century, old sailors swapped stories about the
ghost continent that lay somewhere far south of the
Indies. In the end they were proved right. When
Abel Tasman returned from his voyage of 1642, the
existence of a large piece of land in that part of the
ocean was no longer a matter of legend. But the mystery of Australis Incognita wasn't really solved until
Captain James Cook formally discovered Australia in
1775 and claimed it for Great Britain.

There are a number of very curious charts on which
we find certain parts of the world definitely located
and outlined hundreds of years before they were actually discovered. In his book *The Maps of Ancient
Sea Kings,* Dr. Charles Hapgood describes Greek
maps that seem to have been the product of detailed
scientific knowledge. They were the sources for later
charts of the globe.

The Greek scholar Eratosthenes not only drew a
map of the world as a sphere, in the third century
B.C., but approximated its diameter and circumference to within 1.3 percent of today's estimates, and
calculated that the continent of the Old World comprised about a third of Earth's circumference, which
also was astonishingly close to the truth. How did Eratosthenes shake free from the dogma of Aristotle, who
taught that Europe was and remained the world?
Aristotle flatly declared that no other continents could
possibly exist, and his authority was almost univer-
sally accepted until well into the Middle Ages.

A remarkable chart drawn in 1513 by a Turkish ad-
miral named Piri Reis came to light in Istanbul in
1929. It clearly showed the contours of North and
South America, and an Antarctica in correct relation
to Europe and Africa. Piri Reis stated on his map that
it was derived from "ancient maps" made in Egypt.
In our Library of Congress are many medieval maps
that are surprisingly accurate delineations of parts of
the world supposedly unknown at the time. The makers of these maps apparently had a precise method of
measuring both latitude and longitude—something
our civilization didn't achieve until the eighteenth
century.

If you grant that there might conceivably have been spacecraft looking down on the oceans and continents, at one or more times in the dim past, and that the beings in the vehicles might have come down and communicated with us groundlings, then at once you see an explanation for the maps and the myths and the rumors that later proved true.

Personally I can't see any other way to explain them, unless I theorize that unrecorded but wide-ranging exploration took place before or during the classical Grecian heyday. Maybe it happened. And maybe a few explorers were whisked onto, or over, the undiscovered lands by friendly astronauts.

This reminded me of the old legends about men who were carried high into the sky by birds under their control. I asked my wife Sally, who is also my ace researcher and authority on mythology, about it. "Aren't there stories containing a description of Earth as it might look from a great height?"

She promptly produced a couple. "Here's one resurrected from early Babylon. It's about Etana, the king of Kish, who had no heir and yearned to ascend into the heavens to find a god who would help him with his problem."

I began reading the translation. *"Etana enlists the aid of an eagle who will fly him. The eagle informs Etana that they will ascend to the place where they are going in a series of rises."* I looked up. "Sounds like the three-stage rocket that puts a spacecraft into orbit."

Glancing through more of the translation, I remarked, "The eagle periodically comments on the land and the sea during various stages of the ascent. Just like an airline pilot trying to entertain the passengers. Listen to this: *'Behold, my friend, the land, how it is. Look upon the sea and the sides of the mountain. Lo, the land becomes a mountain and the sea is turned to waters of—'* The fragment of the tablet stops there."

Sally said, "Remember your talks with Scott Carpenter? He said that the view from even the highest mountaintops wasn't like the view from a spacecraft."

I went to a filing cabinet and pulled out a transcript of one of my interviews with him. " 'One thing that struck me was the preponderance of ocean and blue,' " I quoted. " 'The farther away you get, the more you see of the ocean.' "

"Like Scott, the eagle and Etana noticed the sea right away," Sally said. "From here on their story gets more technical. The time that it takes to make the ascent is given as a double march. That's a distance measurement that a warrior-king would probably be familiar with."

"Well, I'm no warrior-king," I said. "How far was a double march?"

"Double time or a forced march would be a speed between four and eight miles an hour, I suppose. In Etana's story, at the end of the first stage of the flight, he and his eagle have climbed a double hour's march.

"Which means they thought they were four to eight miles high. An interesting detail. If Etana really had a ride with astronauts from another world, it's the sort of detail they would mention to him. Well, let's see what else he says. After three more double hour's marches the sea looks *like the canal of a gardener*, whatever that means."

Sally said, "Maybe a drainage ditch, or an irrigation canal? I guess one of the smaller seas could look fairly narrow. Here in Scott Carpenter's transcript he says, 'In Earth orbit you're close enough so that you can see only Africa when you're over it, just about, and you see the green of the jungle, the brown of the desert.' Maybe Etana just saw a narrow strip of ocean at the edge, during that part of his orbit."

"The legend goes on to tell how Etana and his eagle arrive *in the plane of the fixed stars*," I said. "The fragments fail here again. But perhaps this is the point where the pull of gravity weakens, and they plot a course for some specific point. By the way, I notice that Etana at this time doesn't want to fly any higher."

"Maybe a little nausea set in from the free fall," Sally said. "It's interesting that whatever Babylonian told this story would know about the possibility of leveling off into an orbital plane."

"But they get another boost and climb some more. Maybe Etana's story got completely garbled as it was handed down through hundreds of retellings. Anyhow, after another double hour's march, the sea appears *'as a cattle yard.'* Later on, the land looks *'like a garden'* and the sea *'like a wicker basket.'"*

"I doubt if anyone could imagine that, if he hadn't seen Earth from the stratosphere," Sally said. "Those terms seem to be fairly adequate descriptions of what Scott Carpenter and other astronauts say they actually saw. And of course we've seen photos they took, so we know too. I think the various land and sea shapes might remind someone of cattle, or a garden, or a wicker basket, if those were familiar to him."

"One more double hour's ascent, and Etana can't distinguish the sea at all," I summarized. "That's exactly the way it was for Scott. See here in his transcript: 'When you get farther away, the general appearance is blue, because it's the water vapor in the air.'"

"Well, it does sound as if somebody might have described an actual flight into the stratosphere," Sally said.

"I agree. How would anyone know that the Earth looks like that from a great height, unless he'd been there? Well, what's the other legend you found, Sally?"

"Maybe it's based on the same experience, because it's supposed to be a tale of Alexander the Great, who spent some time in Babylon. According to history, while he was there he surrounded himself with priests and magicians."

"Was he supposedly launched on his flight from Babylon?"

"Nobody knows. Pictures and engravings of his ascension have been found on Greek walls, Roman walls, and others ranging through Coptic and Armenian and Syrian to prehistoric French. They show him flying, but not launching."

"Are there any descriptions or portrayals of what he allegedly saw during the flight?"

"Some." She looked through her notes. "Reports from various sources go something like this. Weeping for new worlds to conquer, Alexander wanted to find the vault of heaven. So he got hold of two enormous birds and didn't feed them for three days. Then he yoked them together and fastened a large basket to the yoke. He sat in the basket and held up a tall pole with a piece of meat fastened to the end. So the birds took off with him, trying to reach the meat."

"Ingenious power system," I said, chuckling. "Almost incredible, isn't it?"

"If he took a flight, I doubt that it was powered in quite that way. But the mythmakers probably couldn't figure any more believable explanation for what happened."

"OK, what's the rest of their story?"

"After a while the air becomes icy cold—"

"Say, that's an interesting fact for someone to imagine," I broke in. "Didn't most cultures believe that the upper air was hotter because it was closer to the Sun?"

"I guess they thought so if they thought about it at all. Icarus's wings supposedly melted, and Phaethon's sky chariot caught fire. Anyway, Alexander is reported to have met a birdman in the stratosphere, who told him he had no business up there."

"That figures," I said. "Careful old pilot warns inexperienced hot pilot."

"I wonder if they were conversing by radio," she said. "No, hardly. They couldn't have known the same language. If ancient astronauts talked with Earth people, it must have been by telepathy. Getting back to Alexander, the story goes that he did get scared and looked down at Earth. He is described as saying that it looked like a threshing floor surrounded by a serpent, which was the sea."

"Another fairly accurate comparison," I said. "In some pictures from spacecraft the sea and clouds do look serpentine. I suppose these legends bring Alexander back to terra firma?"

"Yes, they do, vaguely. If he managed a soft land-ing—actually, I mean, not mythically—then he came down in a more sophisticated spacecraft than any yet built by America or Russia. The story seems to indi-cate that he landed seven days' march away from his camp, and nearly starved getting back."

The more I thought about the legends, the more I remembered that the idea of man's ability to fly as well as his need to fly has appeared over and over again in every culture, including western civilization. Where does this impulse come from? Why is the need to fly such a perennial obsession?

In almost every age there was someone who was so sure he could fly that he staked his life on it. Had they seen or heard something that convinced them it could be done? Or did all the legends of flying men have something to do with it?

Simon, a black magician of Nero's time, flew to his death in the Roman Forum. Ismahud, a Saracen, tried to fly before one of the Byzantine emperors, Comnenus, and broke himself up at the foot of a tower. In the Dark Ages there was Oliver, a Malmes-bury monk, who threw himself from a rooftop with wings made of framework and cloth. Leonardo da Vinci had a pupil named Danti who tried out his master's flying machine and died. There was a medieval French locksmith named Besnier; and Juan Torto of Portugal; and Kaspar Mohr, the Flying Priest of Württemberg.

At the beginning of the sixteenth century Father John Damien jumped from the wall of Stirling Castle with wings made of hens' feathers, and lived to talk about it. There was Berblinger, the little flying tailor of Ulm. And Louis Pierre Mouillard, the poet. And a Captain Jean Marie le Bris. And someone named De Bacqueville. Then finally in 1853 the English inventor Sir George Cayley built a glider that carried a small boy successfully. And in 1896 the German engineer Otto Lilienthal built a glider that would carry a man—but he crashed to his death too.

All these men were deluded, in a way. But I won-der if there was some shred of fact behind their belief that flying was possible. Maybe there was talk, far back somewhere, about men who really had flown—like the talk about men with faces on their chests, or the talk about Prester John. Did you know that detailed plans for a powered airplane have been found in an ancient Sanskrit scroll?

Then too, man's early religions always seemed to include gods who could vault through the air or come down out of the clouds. I've seen hundreds on hundreds of museum carvings and paintings that depict god figures with wings and bird bodies, or sometimes bird heads, or headdresses that could be space helmets.

If a so-called god were never seen without his flight equipment, then people would think it was part of him, or his regular costume—and it would be included in the carvings and pictures of him made long afterward.

Something Carl Jung wrote may explain how a sudden surprising event gets reshaped and rationalized and distorted almost out of recognition as it's handed down by word of mouth through the generations: "Because there are innumerable things beyond the range of human understanding, we constantly use symbolic terms to represent concepts that we cannot fully comprehend."

In other words, if primitive people saw an aviator or an astronaut come down from the skies, they'd probably tell their friends that he had wings or rode in a flaming chariot, to make it more believable. They certainly couldn't describe a futuristic spacecraft.

Before Africa was discovered, all reasonable men said it was sheer superstition to believe the legends of a terrible land down near the equator somewhere, a place where the sun turned men permanently black. Even when the first reports of black natives in Africa and Australia came in, scholars and savants still scoffed.

We tend to believe what we want to believe. It's hard to face isolated unexplained facts if they conflict with our mental picture of the world. We ourselves may be victims of mental blocks that will seem ridiculous to people a thousand years from now.

# XIV

## *How Did Man Get His Brain?*

Evolution is the biggest story of all. The story of
how life kept climbing through hundreds of millions
of years and as many million forms and shapes of organisms, from a world populated by single-celled
creatures to the emergence of billion-celled brains, is
the tale that surpasses every other speculation, saga,
and melodrama.

It is the grand design in which every other event
and adventure is merely a detail. Not only is it the
tallest of all tall stories ever told, it is certainly the
most wonderful. And, finally, it is so gripping because
it is our tale.

We human beings are its latest few words, perhaps
its climax. Just to piece together our story's tentative
outline, a hundred and fifty years of worldwide study
have been needed. Vast sections are still lacking. And
there is still hot debate about how the parts we've
found should really fit together. A number of experts
fail to agree why all animals, except man, are so specialized that there seems little hope of their future
advance.

Man might be called the least specialized of all living creatures—the great generalist. This makes him a
mystery to evolutionists.

Nobody knows why one stock, our own, is still
struggling to become stronger, wiser, more aware.
Some experts often remind us of our bestial past. But
most of us know in our innermost being that we have

to keep choosing and striving. We have to transcend our fears, our greed, and our laziness. We have to keep fanning the spark of our wonder, our will to understand and to cooperate. Our most encouraging sign of health is the fact that we are still capable sometimes of creeping outside the thickening crust of our technological accomplishment to gaze around us with a sense of dissatisfaction and aspiration.

This trait that is so deeply true of our species—may it not be bred in us? May it be an essence we inherited from superhuman ancestors and so, in some way, be part of their experience? All my exploration and study while producing "In Search of Ancient Mysteries" kept thrusting my nose into this great question.

So I looked back through anthropology books—which have a way of becoming outdated very fast—to review the theory of evolution as it applied (or didn't apply altogether?) to mankind.

Until 1859 almost everyone believed that animals and plants never changed and that all living things had appeared on Earth in exactly the same forms that they have at present. Then the British naturalist Charles Darwin published a book that revolutionized the science of biology, and shook our belief in the biblical tale of Genesis.

This book, *On the Origin of Species by Means of Natural Selection,* was a long-lasting sensation. Its first edition sold out in a day. It outlined the theory that all today's creatures evolved from early, different species.

Darwin based his theory on three central observations. 1. All members within a species vary. Some are taller than their fellows, some are faster, some have keener eyesight or thicker necks or longer claws. 2. Most creatures produce large numbers of offspring—more than will survive. The weaker die young. 3. Those that survive and breed are, statistically speaking, those whose variations give them an advantage. They represent the "survival of the fittest," because they are the most cleverly adapted to their environment.

Over thousands of generations, offspring inherit and

in turn enhance the genetic endowment they receive. Thus endless slow changes give rise to new species.

The evidence for evolution was overwhelming. Fossils kept a billion-year record of changes in creatures. A study of embryos showed primitive structures even in today's highly evolved animals. Our own bodies contained vestigial organs that were clear signs of youthful apprenticeship in the waters and trees. Biologists compared similar structures in groups of related animals, and deduced which ones shared a common branch of life's family tree. Finally in the 1950s the new science of molecular biology, with its epochal discovery of how DNA carries the genetic code of the chromosomes, went far to show us how the machinery of genetic inheritance works.

However, Darwin's theory and all the evidence for it didn't account for one mysterious and comparatively recent gap in the long record of life's evolving and proliferating.

Through three billion years the story of evolution had been an epic of changing equipment: clutching burr and grasping claw and groping root, struggling upward eternally. Life had been shaped by the lifeless world's blind forces. In all that prehuman world had been no creature capable of thinking back or ahead. Forms of life had only the will to crawl, to find the crevice, the niche, the nest on this mountain of inanimate matter. No living creature had wept above another's grave.

Then a small soundless explosion occurred.

Within the thick-walled skull of a ground-dwelling ape, a little packet of sluggish gray matter was sparked into glowing life. It began to expand at a remarkable rate.

The mutation took place in silence, the silence of some great fungus coming up at night in a forest glade. That dread organ that was to unlock the wild powers of the universe and yet teach us all we know of compassion and love was growing quickly under a small dome of bone. Something apparently unpredictable had triggered this growth.

How did man get his brain?

Darwin's great contemporary Alfred Russel Wallace, codiscoverer with him of the principle of natural selection, propounded that simple question in 1869. The question has bothered evolutionists ever since. Receiving his copy of Wallace's article raising the question, Darwin wrote "NO!" in the margin, triple scored and showered with exclamation points.

Darwin saw in the sudden growth of man's unique brain only the undirected play of such natural selection as had created the rest of the swarming world of organisms. Wallace thought that human intellect could only be explained by the direct intervention of some cosmic force.

Darwin eventually admitted that his principle of limited perfection—that is, the idea that life could evolve only enough to survive in competition with other life or to adjust to changes in environment—had been oddly upset in the case of man. He had said that an organ, such as an eye or a digestive system, could reach perfection only for a given purpose in a given environment. To explain how mankind managed by natural selection to acquire a brain that far surpassed all other brains, Darwin had to assume a long struggle of man with man and tribe with tribe.

But archaeologists found little evidence of primate-versus-primate strife, and no human fossils showing gradual stages of evolution. For a period of two million years the story of primates is told only by a few handfuls of broken bones and teeth. To make it harder, these fossils are from places thousands of miles apart.

Consequently an abyss yawned between man and ape. Darwinians tried to minimize it by throwing modern native tribes into the gap as living "missing links" in the ladder of human ascent. They would soon be extinct because their brains were subhuman, the theorists held.

This seemed logical enough to Victorians. They thought that "lesser breeds without the law" must be biologically inferior to the white man, incapable of ever rising to the majesty of an umbrella and a top hat. Indeed some races were erroneously considered as only slightly above apes, perhaps uttering only grunts or chattering like monkeys.

It was just at this time that Wallace raised his lonely protest. He had spent years among natives in tropical islands, and he knew that their simple food-gathering way of life had never required much brain-power—yet their native intelligence was surprisingly high. He wrote:

> The mental requirements of the lowest savages such as the Australians or the Andaman Islanders are very little above those of many animals. . . . How, then, was an organ developed so far beyond the needs of its possessor?
>
> Natural selection could only have endowed the savage with a brain a little superior to that of an ape, whereas he actually possesses one but very little inferior to that of the average members of our learned societies. . . . An instrument has been developed in advance of the needs of its possessor.

Going further, Wallace challenged the Darwinian view of man by pointing out that artistic, mathematical, and musical abilities couldn't be accounted for by the struggle to survive or by adjustment to the environment. Something else, he insisted, some unknown spiritual element, had to be at work in the elaboration of the human brain.

"I differ grievously from you and am very sorry for it," Darwin retorted. But he offered no valid answer to Wallace's objections. He merely fired off a few remarks about the inherited effects of habit—a contention now discredited by science. This seemed enough. The scientific establishment slowly forgot Wallace's challenge and settled into a great complacency.

But the awkward question that Wallace asked has returned to haunt us.

We learned that primeval man never arose in the remote regions of Australia and South America. He only reached them by migration. These continents existed under the same sun and were surrounded by the same waters as our own. If man arose so naturally, was so easy to produce, why did two great continental laboratories of evolution fail to produce him?

So it begins to appear that the human emergence may not have been inevitable. Perhaps, as Wallace thought, some "higher force" took a hand.

Moreover, archaeological discoveries have now taken us far, far back into the youth of mankind without showing us the link between him and other primates. We now know that man is much older than we thought.

After three decades on hands and knees combing the fossil-rich prehistoric lake beds of East Africa, the British archaeologists Louis S. B. Leakey and his wife Mary found the fossilized skull of an unmistakably manlike creature. Through the ages the pressure of the rock bed had cracked his cranium into more than four hundred fragile shreds. The Leakeys spent a year putting it together—a task like reassembling an eggshell run over by a truck, as another archaeologist put it.

They christened their find *Zinjanthropus* ("East African man," using the Arabic word for East Africa). Its name shrank to a familiar *Zinj* among scientists. *Zinj* was remarkable for two reasons.

First, he was found among clearly shaped stone tools. Thus *Zinj* wasn't merely a user of chance things that came to hand; he was a thinker who shaped. Second, in 1961 the University of California's new potassium-argon dating process indicated that *Zinj* had been in his rocky coffin for nearly two million years!

If the university's "clock" of radioactivity is correct, the history of stone-using man will have been carried back almost a million years before the Ice Age.

*Zinj*'s head was so different from that of modern man that if he were alive today, scrubbed and shaved and dressed, we might draw back in alarm. His face didn't have a pronounced muzzle like an ape's. It was flattish and spade shaped, with a massive jaw good for cracking bones. His forehead sloped back so abruptly that it seemed squashed in—and consequently his braincase was less than half the size of ours.

His thoughts were nearly all hunches or happy accidents. But he did think, and he was unlike other forms of life in another way. They had adapted to environment. He was generalized. He was without tusks or talons, scales, wings, spurs, spines, or stings. Instead of running on all fours, which would have helped him avoid natural enemies, he stood up almost straight. He was slow afoot and slow in the trees if he climbed at all. How strange that he survived!

His prehistoric campsite shows no evidence of burning or charring, so it seems that *Zinj* was not a fire user. Almost certainly he could not talk.

After *Zinj*—that first glimpse of something at least subhuman in the record of geologic strata—there isn't another fragment of manlike bone in view for an interval of at least one million years.

In between are traces of crude stone tools that hint that some form of *Genus Homo* was present on three continents in the earlier half of the Ice Age. But to the anthropologist it is like peering through fog. Here and there, amid blank areas of hundreds of thousands of years, he thinks he sees a shambling figure, or a half-wild primordial face staring out through some momentary opening. But he sees no sign that *Genus Homo* was progressing.

Not until he reaches a time about a million years ago does he see another fossil that could be human. This one was in a cave near Peking.

The clues indicate that here a Stone Age hunter had enough foresight to batter a rock into a useful shape, and to carry it with him when he went hunting. More significant, he had learned the great trick of carrying a little tongue of the sun with him to ward off beasts and warm his cave.

Peking man's regular use of fire, as the anthropologist F. Clark Howell says, implies a creature "provident enough to keep supplies of fuel on hand and skillful enough to keep fires going." Still, if the million years between *Zinj* and Peking man had brought only that much progress, surely one more million would not be enough to put him where he is today.

In his monumental *Story of Civilization,* the great historian Will Durant admits:

> Immense volumes have been written to expound our knowledge, and conceal our ignorance, of primitive man. . . . Primitive cultures were not necessarily the ancestors of our own; for all we know they may be the degenerate remnants of higher cultures that decayed when human leadership moved in the wake of the receding ice.
>
> . . . If we accept the precarious theories of contemporary science, the creature who became man by learning to speak was one of the adaptable species that survived from those frozen centuries. In the Interglacial Stages, while the ice was retreating (and, for all we know, long before) this strange organism discovered fire, developed the art of fashioning weapons and tools, and thereby paved the way to civilization.

This gives some scholarly respectability to the idea I've put forward throughout this book: the idea that visits and/or seeding at long intervals by an advanced race from outside our solar system may be the cause of man's sudden great leaps forward followed by long periods of stagnation or regression.

Let's see how this thesis fits the known facts about manlike creatures as we've traced their development thus far.

*Zinj* and Peking man were both small-brained hominids. In the long, long interval between them, there was little change in the skull size or body structure of the species.

However, as Dr. Durant pointed out, during the interglacial stages somebody made a revolutionary technological discovery: the use of fire. Maybe this intellectual feat happened in the natural course of evolution, although no other living creatures ever made such a discovery.

But maybe, on the other hand, somebody dropped in from the skies and taught the submen about fire. And still another maybe—maybe a colony of advanced beings lived on Earth for thousands of years during one of those dim interglacial stages, and then had to leave when the next Ice Age came to grind away all traces of the colony. The one heritage—lasting heritage, anyway—that they were able to leave the Earthlings could have been the ability to capture fire, keep it alive, carry it with them, and put it where it would help them.

Degenerate descendants of the little colony of astronauts could have been the Neanderthals—the next known type of *Homo*, and a surprisingly different type than *Zinj* and Peking man. To me it isn't inconceivable that the Neanderthals could be the long-afterward result of a mingling of astronauts' seeds with those of the earlier hominids.

At least we can be fairly sure that the Neanderthals weren't swingers in trees like their supposed ancestors the apes. This type's hand and foot, according to anatomists, are too different to have been made over from an arboreal ancestor's in a few hundred thousand years.

Neanderthal got his name because a skull and bones of this type were first dug up in the Neanderthal Valley of the German Rhineland. Since then the remains of 155 very similar hominids have been found in sixty-eight sites scattered over Europe, the Near East, and elsewhere. So we have a detailed and consistent picture of the Neanderthals.

They were short and thickset, averaging a little taller than five feet. But here's the fact that makes me suspect an infusion of very different seeds: Their low skull vaults had a cranial capacity of sixteen hundred cubic centimeters—more than one and one-half times that of the *Zinj* and Peking types, and two hundred cubic centimeters greater than our own!

Pioneer paleontologists pictured the Neanderthals as barrel-chested, hairy, slow-moving, chinless, and brutish. But we now deduce that they had no more body hair than we do (when they lost it, and why, is another mystery) and that they weren't always dull brutes.

Today's experts are more inclined to think that if we gave a Neanderthal a shave and haircut, and dressed him in well-fitting clothes, he might walk down New York's Fifth Avenue without getting many second glances.

Neanderthal man showed a good deal of foresight. He skinned animals, scraped off the superfluous flesh, then strained and pulled and pegged out the skin flat on the grass. When it dried, he wore it to keep himself warm.

He made not only tools, but also tools to make future tools: sawlike blades for cutting wood or bone; chisels and scrapers; notched blades set between two handles, presumably for smoothing the round handles of spears. He probably used a variety of wooden implements too. Of course all those have long since rotted away.

We know that the Neanderthals were right-handed like modern men, because the left side of the brain (which serves the right side of the body) is bigger than the right. But while the back parts of the brain, which control sight and touch and bodily agility are well developed, the front parts, which are connected with thought and speech, are comparatively small. Their brains were as big as ours, but different. This *Homo* had certainly a very different mentality from *Homo sapiens,* as we choose to call ourselves.

On the other hand, long study has shown us that Neanderthal man had his own small dreams and kindnesses. He fed and sheltered the lame and maimed among his kind. He buried his dead in niches scooped out of the dirt and walled by rock slabs.

One of the best-known Neanderthal skeletons is that of a youth who apparently had been laid away with real tenderness. He was placed in a sleeping posture, head on forearm. His head lay on flint fragments carefully piled together to make a pillow.

Somewhere along the way, the Neanderthals evidently learned to believe in an afterlife. (Did superhuman visitors give them this idea?) Most of their graves contained an ax and other tools that someone must have thought would later be useful to them.

More touching yet, in one grave were found clusters of flower pollen from at least eight kinds of flowers—small, bright kinds. No accident of nature could have put them so deep in the cave where the skeleton was found. Someone in the last Ice Age, it seems, had ranged over the mountainside with the mournful task of collecting flowers for the dead.

The Neanderthals may have wandered, squatted about their fires in their caves, and died in Europe for a period extending over eighty thousand years. In all that time they altered little, if we can believe the evidence.

And by about 35,000 B.C. they disappeared entirely, as far as we can tell. No more recent skeletons of the Neanderthal type have ever been found. To the end they were low-browed, as if their thick skulls imprisoned their brains.

Next came another type of creature: Cro-Magnon man, as different from the Neanderthals as those had been from their known precursors. There is no trace of any intermixture between Cro-Magnons and Neanderthals, whose beetle brows and thick necks and squat stature may have seemed repulsively strange to the newcomers. Sir Harry Johnson, a British anthropologist, hazards an interesting guess: "The dim racial remembrance of such gorillalike monsters, with cunning brains, shambling gait, strong teeth, and possibly cannibalistic tendencies, may be the germ of the ogre in folklore."

Discoveries during the last thirty years have shown that Darwin's simplified version of single-line human evolution is very unlikely to be true. Most anthropologists now think that the Neanderthal represents a "dead-end" branch of mankind's family tree.

Nevertheless he left us the first evidences of man's social and religious sensibilities. Long ridiculed and disdained as a symbol of subhuman brutality, he now seems worthy of being regarded at least as our cousin. For which of us would refuse to acknowledge a relative who laid his dead to rest with offerings and flowers?

Whether it was his own heavy brow that changed in the chill nights, or that somewhere his line mingled with a changeling brood who multiplied at his expense, or that he died off or was killed off, we have no way of knowing. We know only that he vanished—and that a strikingly different breed, which we call *Homo sapiens* or Cro-Magnon (from the discovery of its relics in a grotto of that name in southern France) appeared on the scene somewhere between 35,000 and 20,000 B.C.

This breed was the progenitor of modern man. He laid the bases of all the civilizations we inherited.

Abundant remains of the same type and age have been dug up all over France, Switzerland, Germany, and Wales. They indicate a people of magnificent vigor and stature, ranging from five feet ten inches to six feet four inches in height. They had narrow sharply cut faces, high foreheads, and astonishingly big brains—their brain capacity ranged from 1590 to 1715 cubic centimeters, as compared with our 1400. Were they from another planet?

It has long been the thought of science, particularly in evolutionary biology, that nature doesn't make great leaps, that her creatures slither in slow disguise from one shape to another. According to this theory, Cro-Magnons must have spent hundreds of centuries acquiring the skills of brain and hand that they possessed when they first came into our ken.

But there is no evidence—either in skulls or artifacts—of this long theoretical transitionary period. The Cro-Magnons seem to have appeared with no warning.

And they didn't change much after they appeared. Man of today, the atomic manipulator, the astronaut who flies faster than sound, has no better brain or body than his ancestors of twenty thousand years ago who replaced the Neanderthals in the caves of Europe. Evolution to all intents and purposes came to a standstill in Cro-Magnon days.

To me, this strongly suggests that the Cro-Magnons were another infusion of seed—or of actual people who came here and bred and colonized. Consider the remarkable evidence of their accomplishments, unaccompanied by any evidence that they built up to these accomplishments gradually:

Using the same raw materials available to their predecessors, they created a brand-new kit of tools. The scraper stone that had the shape of a shell became a shovel or a hoe. The rough stone became a file. The round stone went into a sling to become a hunting weapon that would survive even classical antiquity.

Using bone, wood, and ivory as well as stone, Cro-Magnon man made polishers, mortars, axes, planes, drills, knives, chisels, choppers, lances, anvils, etchers, fishhooks, harpoons, wedges, awls, pins, and doubtless many more.

He had lamps to carry with him into the depths of caves; there are shallow bowls ground from soapstone that held the grease he burned to give him light. Of course caves may not have been his only dwellings. (Cro-Magnons, like Neanderthals, are known to us as "cave men" because their remains are found in caves. But it may be one of time's jokes that only those who lived in caves, or died in them, have transmitted their bones to archaeologists.)

He had the unprecedented ability to keep track of events and thereby remind himself when to expect their recurrence. Thousands of notational sequences have been found on engraved bones and stones dating as far back as thirty thousand years. These markings puzzled archaeologists for a century.

Recently, though, Alexander Marshack of Harvard has shown that these curious notations must have served as a kind of farmer's almanac tied in with a lunar calendar. Some are illustrated with little picture drawings representing natural events, so that whoever kept the bone or stone could know when to expect the changes of the seasons and the movement or dispersal of game.

Strange to relate, we know Cro-Magnon man best by his art.

There is one little ivory head of a girl with an elaborate coiffure. Figures have been found modeled in clay, although no people in the Ice Age made any use of pottery. Fairly delicate sewing must have been done, because bone needles have been found that one authority says were "much superior to those of later, even historical, times, down to the Renaissance. The Romans, for example, never had needles comparable to those of this epoch."

One afternoon in the summer of 1879, amateur archaeologist Marcelino de Sautuola came upon a large cave on his estate at Altamira, in northern Spain. For thousands of years the entrance had been hermetically sealed by fallen rocks that stalagmite deposits had cemented. But now the ancient entrance had been opened by blasting for new construction. He began digging in the rubble at its mouth.

One day his five-year-old daughter accompanied him. Not compelled like her father to stoop as she walked through the cave, she could look up at the ceiling. Suddenly she cried, "Toros! Toros! Papa, come quickly!" He dropped his pick and scrambled into the cavern where she stood in the half light, pointing at the ceiling.

When he crouched and raised his lantern, Don Marcelino felt his skin prickle. He saw not bulls but prehistoric bison, magnificently painted in shades of brown, red, yellow, and black.

There were seventeen of them in incredibly lifelike poses—standing, pawing the ground, falling wounded, rolling in the dust, or curled in sleep.

Exploring deeper in the cave, he found dozens of other animals pictured on walls and ceilings: a wonderful delicate hind, giant cattle, great-antlered stags, charging wild boar.

The pictures had remained through thousands of years as fresh and glowing as on the day they were created. Their colors adhered to Don Marcelino's fingertip when he touched them.

The old grandee fell victim to the enchantment of these magic Ice Age paintings. He knew they had to be very ancient. Most of the animals so vividly depicted were long since extinct, or had disappeared from western Europe thousands of years earlier. And he had unearthed from the cave's entrance exactly the kind of tools already discovered in Cro-Magnon caves of France: bodkins, scrapers, rasps, sewing needles—

all the implements associated with a well-appointed
Ice Age home.

Don Marcelino devoted the rest of his life to the
service of the cave. When he published a report in
1880, archaeologists read it with genial skepticism. A
few did him the honor to visit Altamira and examine
the paintings, only to pronounce them a hoax. Never,
said the learned men, could such superb art have
been created by savages. Don Marcelino himself was
accused of having hired some fine artist to forge the
paintings, perhaps as a plot to discredit the "new
science" of prehistory. The Congress of Prehistorians
at Lisbon unanimously condemned him. He died an
object of ridicule in 1888.

The perfectly reasonable incredulity persisted for
twenty years. Then the French archaeologist Henri
Breuil, who was to win acclaim as the "priest of the
painted caves," found similar art in caves generally
conceded to be prehistoric because of their contents
of unpolished flint tools and polished ivory and bone.

Thereafter more than a hundred caves decorated
with Old Stone Age paintings, engravings, and sculpture were found—in Spain, France, Italy, and the
Ural Mountains, which lie between Europe and Asia.
Prehistorians finally conceded that the artists must
have lived in the late Paleolithic (Old Stone) Age
when Cro-Magnons were numerous.

In 1940 a band of schoolboys near Lascaux, in
France, slid down a rocky chute into a cavern that
proved to be a painted menagerie of prehistoric
beasts. Among the lively figures in this Louvre of
"primitive" art were prodigious bulls thirteen to seventeen feet long; galloping ponies; woolly mammoths;
exquisite black-and-yellow "Chinese horses" (so-called
because they resembled ones painted by the highly
refined Tang dynasty in China); a frieze of antlered
stags swimming a river; a mythical monster with a
hippopotamus body and long straight horns. Here was
life, action, nobility conveyed overwhelmingly with
two or three brave lines; here a single stroke (or did
others fade?) created a living charging beast.

Taken altogether, the Cro-Magnon paintings were

of such skill and delicacy as to suggest the unhappy thought that art, in this field at least, hadn't advanced much in the whole course of civilized history. These paintings were the very first trace of human artistry; how could they be so expert?

They raised another question too—the same question Wallace had asked long ago. Why and how did man suddenly begin to live a strange rich mental life, with artistic aspects that had little use in the supposedly brutal struggle for survival? From what did his talent evolve?

We don't know how art began any more than we know how language started. Painting is a sophisticated art, presuming many centuries of mental and technical development. If we accept current theory (which it is always dangerous to do), we think that painting developed from carving. Painting is statuary minus a dimension. And there are plenty of good examples of Cro-Magnon skill in carving.

In one cave in France were several ornamental handles carved from reindeer antlers; one is of such excellent workmanship that art critics think the sculptor had generations of tradition and development behind him. Stone statues of a wild horse, a reindeer, and a mammoth have been dug up in Czechoslovakia among remains dated roughly at 30,000 B.C.

Dr. Durant admits puzzlement:

The whole interpretation of history as progress falters when we consider that these statues and paintings, numerous though they are, may be but an infinitesimal fraction of the art that expressed or adorned the life of primitive man. What remains is found in caves, where the elements were in some measure kept at bay; it does not follow that prehistoric men were artists only when in caves. They may have carved as sedulously and ubiquitously as the Japanese, and may have fashioned statuary as abundantly as the Greeks. They may have painted not only rocks in caverns, but textiles, wood, everything. They may have created masterpieces far superior to the fragments that survive.

We know something of how they worked. The first step was to scratch a rough sketch with a pointed piece of flint. We have the "first draft" for one Alta-mira picture—a very lively representation of hinds, on a slab of stone. Another first draft tells us something more surprising, perhaps, than the paintings them-selves.

In 1903 prehistorians found the wall picture of a mighty old bison, drawn with great individuality in a cave at Font-de-Gaume in the Dordogne, France. In 1926 a slab of slate was found 188 miles away in an-other cave. It bore the sketch from which the wall picture at Font-de-Gaume had been painted.

We must conclude that the mere sketch, only sug-gested in outline and still without color, was so highly prized that some Cro-Magnon kept it at home—kept it so carefully that it survived ten or maybe twenty thousand years.

Was there already an art trade in those days? Prob-ably we'll never know. But we can deduce, from the distance traveled by this materially worthless artifact, that tens of thousands of years ago the Cro-Magnons made long journeys. Isn't it strange, and moving, that a journey was made not just for food or utilitarian ob-jects, but for an insignificant-looking slate covered with scratches?

Cro-Magnon artists may actually have gone to school to develop their talent. At Limeuil, in south-western France, 137 stone sketch slabs were found, many of them poorly executed, with details often cor-rected as if by a teacher's hand. In one grotto a tube was discovered, made from reindeer bones and filled with pigment. In another a stone palette was still thick with red ocher paint after two hundred cen-turies.

Cro-Magnon painters had no greens or blues, but got black and violet-black colors from manganese ox-ides. They may have made black pigments from char-coal or the soot of burnt fat. The brown, yellow, or-ange, and red hues came from iron ore, which the painters or their assistants ground to powder between stones, then mixed with animal blood, plant juices, or animal fat. Sometimes the ocher was mixed with tallow and rolled into crayons.

The painters laid on their colors thickly in a variety of ways—with brushes made of fur or feathers or the chewed end of a twig; with compressed lichen and moss; with fingertips; or by blowing them onto the wall through hollow bones or reeds.

Whatever the method, the figures were usually painted in bold sure strokes, with few signs of correction. Apparently the arts were highly developed and widely practiced eighteen thousand years ago. Maybe there were full-time artists paid in food or furs by art lovers; maybe there were Bohemians starving in the less respectable caves.

With the retreat of the last great glaciers, around 10,000 B.C., the cave art of the Old Stone Age seems to have ended abruptly. No doubt people moved out of the caverns as the climate warmed, and made wooden shelters along rivers and lakes. Thereafter they learned to cultivate crops and to domesticate animals. They roamed more widely. By the time the first traders from the eastern Mediterranean reached western Europe, around 1800 B.C., the most recent cave paintings were some nine thousand years old. The skills, the styles, and the inspiration that had created them were long forgotten. The first and one of the greatest eras of artistic expression had passed forever. But civilization, as we know it, was just dawning.

What a paradox.

Civilization is social order promoting cultural creation. It begins where chaos and insecurity end. Certain factors can encourage civilization, or impede it. Ice, for example. Civilization is an interlude between ice ages. At times the great cold may come again, covering the works of man with glaciers and stone, pushing civilization into a few small corners of the planet. Or the demons of volcanos and earthquakes, by whose leave we build our cities, may twitch and consume us indifferently. Or huge floods may wash us away.

Who knows how many past civilizations, tens of

thousands of years ago, were utterly destroyed by advancing ice or lava or water? Space colonies could have come and gone at fifty-thousand-year intervals, and we'd have no way of knowing—although we might suspect it, from the hints of abrupt changes in mankind that I've just sketched.

"We cannot properly estimate the achievements of prehistoric man," Dr. Durant writes. "We suspect that time has destroyed remains that would narrow the gap between primeval and modern man."

Another distinguished scientist and thoughtful teacher, Loren Eiseley (chairman of the anthropology department at the University of Pennsylvania) has suspicions too. He often writes of "what I choose to call the 'unnatural' aspect of man; unnatural, that is, in the sense that there is nothing else like it on the planet. ... Though theories abound, we know little about why man became man at all. He is an inconceivably rare and strange beast. There has been no previous evolutionary novelty comparable to this save the act of creation itself. Man, imperfect transitory man, carries within him some uncanny spark from the first lightning that split the void. He alone can walk straight-footed to his own death and hold the world well lost for the sake of such intangible things as truth and love."

Putting it more bluntly, two modern biologists, M. R. A. Chance and A. P. Mead, wrote a symposium paper that confessed, "No adequate explanation has been put forward to account for so large a cerebrum as that found in man."

Our mysterious cerebrum is worth considering further. If man's brain—a brain more than twice as large as his much bigger relative the gorilla—is to be acquired in infancy, it can't be grown during the nine months before birth. If it took place in the embryo, man literally couldn't be born. Even as it is, an infant's head is one of the factors making human birth comparatively difficult. Yet his brain size at birth is only slightly bigger than a baby gorilla's.

In the first year of life a human child's brain triples in size. This amazing leap, unlike anything else we know in the animal world, gives man his uniquely human qualities.

The child brain is strangely plastic, quick to learn from the world around it—unlike animals' brains, which arrive full of instincts and need to learn little. (Even in the highest forms of invertebrates—the social insects—behavior is governed almost entirely by instinct. Learning plays a small part.) The human brain must learn by experience.

Here we see another mysterious difference between mankind and other kinds: childhood.

A human baby has a peculiar larval helplessness, which should doom him to quick extinction if "survival of the fittest" were the sole law of life. His periods of helpless infancy and childhood are much longer than those of any other creature. He must assimilate a huge store of information and ways of behavior from the social group into which he is born. He must master the magic tool of language.

All this poses greater challenges to *Homo sapiens* than to any other species. Through hundreds of thousands of years, mankind's family bonds had to hold beyond seasonal matings. Instead of the casual sex life of most animals, there had to be a semipermanent family.

Family life is slightly different in separate societies, but it is always and everywhere ennobled by its tender and continuing care of the human offspring through the lengthened period of childhood. Without the willingness of fallible, loving adults to spend years nursing their little ones, man would long since have vanished from the Earth.

The biggest mystery in the development of living organisms is this unique adjustment of family relationship to protect infancy. Only in one group of creatures—that giving rise to man—has it been successfully developed in the three billion years or so that life has existed here.

Man exists because of a love more continuing than in any other form of life. This fact underlies everything else about him. What else but love, altruism, and wisdom have brought us even this pitiful distance on the human journey?

Yet man also has uniquely evil qualities: coldly calculated cruelty, avarice, arrogance, lust for power—are these found in other animals?

The human brain, magnificent as it is, still bears within itself an older and lower brain—you might call it a fossil remnant—geared to help a creature struggling to become human, and dragged with him, sadly, out of the darkness.

We still carry that tiny vesicular forebrain, with its traits that once kept us alive. Traits like fear of the stranger, when the stranger was two eyes in the dark beyond the fire. Aggression, sharpened by nature in two million years of wandering the wastes of an open world. Flashes of unreasoning temper, frustrations, occasional irrationalities that are echoes out of an older bestial machine.

Indeed, it has been suggested that the enlargement of the human brain has gone so fast and so far that the result is actually pathological. The great Hungarian novelist and essayist Arthur Koestler wrote an article in 1968 with the title, "Is Man's Brain an Evolutionary Mistake?" He pointed out that a seemingly muddled nature has provided man with three brains: one reptilian, one lower mammalian, and his own phenomenal higher mammalian brain. They don't get along with one another.

"If the evidence had not taught us the contrary," he wrote, "we would expect an evolutionary development that gradually transformed the primitive old brain into a more sophisticated instrument—as it transformed claw into hand, gill into lung. Instead evolution superimposed a new, superior structure on an old one, with partly overlapping functions and without providing the new with a clear-cut control over the old."

Maybe it wasn't, strictly speaking, all evolution. Maybe this phenomenon of one brain superimposed on another could be the result of subhuman Earthlings interbred with highly refined men from another planet.

If so, we know that those other-worldly people must have been noble, creative, and above all loving.

The better side of our human nature could be a gift from them. In the Middle Ages man was called *Homo duplex*—a thing half of flesh and half of spirit. The term well expresses our predicament and our hope.

Neurologists say that the most recently acquired and less specialized regions of the brain, the "silent areas," mature last. Maybe they haven't all matured yet. With good reason, some brain specialists believe that here may lie other potentialities that only the race's future may reveal. Perhaps we hold within ourselves wonders greater than we yet know.

Then too, if help has come from outside in ages past, it may come again. Whether we speak of a god come down to Earth or a man inspired toward god, the dream is great.

# XV

## Shortcuts in Space-Time?

A puzzle in the background bothered me during the whole time I was shaping up "In Search of Ancient Mysteries" as a television documentary and as a book. Perhaps the same puzzle bothered you.

That puzzle is the hypothetical other-worldly spacecraft. How do they come and go?

I don't think it's enough to say merely, "Oh, they must have a fantastic power system so they travel at nearly the speed of light."

Even at the speed of light, a vehicle from the solar system nearest to ours would need at least eight years for each round trip. The next-closest stars would require twenty to forty years, as I indicated in Chapter 2.

Nor am I completely satisfied to say, with Einstein, that the trip would seem much shorter to cosmonauts because time would slow down for them. Time really does decelerate inside a vehicle traveling at great speed; experiments have proven this. A trip lasting decades in planet time might be only a day or week of cosmonaut time. But the spacemen starting for Earth would have to say good-bye to their own generation. If they returned, still young, they would find their contemporaries older by decades, or dead.

Maybe a dedicated missionary-type adventurer would be willing to cut loose from his own world. Perhaps only a few have been needed in the whole billion years of our planet's existence. But if so, we need some other explanation for those 440 unexplained sightings of strange craft in our sky within one decade or so; for all those large lighted objects seen appearing, disappearing, and reappearing every few years throughout the nineteenth and twentieth centuries; for the remarkably accurate yet ancient world maps apparently made from the air, as I mentioned in chapter 13.

I can't quite visualize a stream of space travelers shuttling between Earth and the nearest habitable planet, if even a quick trip means coming back to a home where everyone has aged twenty years.

I don't say it's impossible. Maybe there are plenty of explorers willing to do it. Maybe some jump at a chance to voyage for centuries in suspended animation.

But the more I think about it, the more I wonder if our visitors take a shortcut.

Maybe they understand the fourth dimension—and even a fifth or sixth dimension—so well that they move around the cosmos in ways we can't see or comprehend.

After all, this is only our twentieth century A.D. and we've already learned that space is curved, thanks to Einstein and others. By our thirtieth or fortieth century, unimagined gateways to hyperspace may have been flung open by geniuses yet unborn.

In an oft-quoted epigram Bertrand Russell says that mathematicians don't have to know what they're talking about. Because of this freedom Bolyai, a Hungarian, and Lobachevski, a Russian, independently figured out new geometries in which space is curved and parallel lines meet. Their colleagues considered them slightly mad. Yet out of this madness came hundreds of concepts of space, one of which proved highly useful in arriving at relativity.

Euclid's classical geometry agrees with our known world only within very narrow limits—in fact, the limits of a drawing board. Extend these limits, and what becomes of our belief that parallel lines can't meet? They meet at the line of the horizon—a simple fact on which all our art perspective is based.

Mathematicians influenced scientific thought profoundly when they developed non-Euclidean geometries based on new ways of thinking about space. Today's scientists visualize the very form of the universe through different eyes. Many are convinced that space must be curved, and time must be curved, as the thinkers like Einstein have said.

Curved space? If we stretch our imagination, we can visualize it. Actually it's easier than imagining the infinite endless space that conventional astronomers used to insist on. Can you imagine a space that has no end? Or can you imagine what could be beyond it?

Let's try an analogy. Suppose you stretch a thin sheet of rubber over the top of a huge kettle. You roll a very light marble over the sheet, and it follows a straight line. But now you fasten several lead weights on the rubber sheet at different points. Their weight dimples it, forming small slopes and hollows. If you roll the marble on this surface, it will no longer roll straight, but will curve toward the slopes and probably fall into one of the hollows.

Think of space as corresponding to the rubber sheet. Think of large gravitational masses like the sun and planets as the lead weights. Think also of any "event"—a beam of light, a spacecraft—as the counterpart of the marble rolling on the membrane. Where there are no masses, space is "flat" and paths of motion are straight. But in the vicinity of large masses space is distorted into curves that affect the path of any object crossing them.

This is what used to be called the force of gravity. But gravitation in Einstein's theory is only an aspect of space. Light rays bent toward the sun "dip" into the slope around it, but have enough zip not to be trapped in the "hollow." A planet circling a sun is riding on the "rim of its hollow" like a cyclist racing around a banked saucer. A spacecraft that gets too deep into the "hollow" will fall toward the mass that causes the hollow.

However, accounting for gravitation in this way forces us to assume that our space is only part of a greater space, just as the rubber sheet is. What we think of as space is probably only as much of it as we can perceive with our limited sensory equipment. It is all around us in a direction toward which we can never point. Our space can't contain it because it contains our space.

Still we can assume it easily enough, as mathematicians do, if we think about it. After all, we assume a three-dimensional universe that we can't really see. We know the Earth isn't flat though it looks so. To our eyes the night sky is just a spangled curtain. Our reasoning mind has transformed it into a fathomless vault sprinkled with fiery balls in ordered motion.

Except for the slight depth perception given by two-eyed vision, our eyesight really shows us only flat moving pictures. And our touch feels only surfaces. What has compelled our intellect to conceive of solid three-dimensional space? Our experience in moving around, above, below, and behind the objects we see.

If somehow we could also have the experience of moving in four dimensions, wouldn't our intellect likewise be compelled to admit the invisible fourth dimension? Even though we can't see it, I think its reality is provable. Geometry and logic are in its favor.

In geometry the point, the line, the plane, and the solid are only mental concepts, although they may have equivalents in the world of objects. The same geometrical relationships continue into regions of which our senses make no report—the higher dimensions.

Lines are bounded by points, and themselves bound planes. Line-bound planes in turn bound solids. What, then, do solids bound? By geometrical logic we must answer, Higher solids: four-dimensional forms invisible to us because we're three-dimensional creatures.

Picture this another way. Visualize a pencil point moving a given distance in an unchanging direction. It traces a line. Move this line at right angles to itself, and it blocks out a rectangle. Move this rectangle at right angles to itself—up or down, that is—and it traces a cube.

Now, for the cube to move at right angles to all its dimensions, a new region of space is needed—a fourth dimension. In such a higher space the cube would trace out a hypercube or tesseract, an imaginary figure so familiar to mathematicians that you'll find it in dictionaries: "A four-dimensional figure bounded by eight cubes, and having twenty-four faces and thirty-two edges."

For a four-dimensional intelligence it's presumably as easy to understand the appearance or disappearance of a vehicle in thin air—or the withdrawal of an orange from its skin without cutting or breaking that skin—as it is for us to see the possibility of taking up a pencil point from the center of a circle and putting it down outside. We don't have to draw our pencil point across the paper to get it out of the circle. Yet the disappearing point would mystify an insect on the paper, living in a two-dimensional flatland, so to speak.

The moment our pencil leaves the flat surface it disappears into the third dimension. This would constitute an occult phenomenon in a world of two dimensions. Correspondingly, a movement into a fourth dimension can explain many phenomena we consider occult in our world.

Could all those ships and aircraft in the Bermuda Triangle have merely been moved into another dimension? Could all those unidentified flying objects come in and out of another dimension?

Some philosophers have sensed a relation between higher dimensions and the occult. Kant wrote, "If it is possible that there are other dimensions of space, it is very probable that God has somewhere produced them. For His works have all the grandeur and variety that can possibly be comprised."

Walt Whitman had a similar thought. "I do not doubt interiors have their interiors, and exteriors their exteriors—and that eyesight has another eyesight, and the hearing another hearing, and the voice another voice."

And five centuries ago an unknown Christian mystic said this about heaven, which his contemporaries assumed to be a definable place: "Heaven is as high down as up, and up as down, behind as before, before as behind, on one side as another. Whoso has a true desire to be at heaven, then that same time he were in heaven. For the high and the next way thither is run by desires and not by paces of feet."

What about merely getting to a far-distant planet instead of to heaven? Can this be done almost instantaneously by people who fully understand curved space and curved time? I think so.

Time is a dimension too. To me it's not exactly a spatial dimension at right angles to all others, but a dimension nevertheless.

It's a dimension because to fix the position of any object you need four coordinates, and one of these is time.

For example, let's suppose I'm trying to find you. If I know that you live on the southwest corner of Second Avenue and Sixty-third Street, let's say, your position is defined in terms of latitude and longitude—that is, in the two dimensions of a plane. Now if on that corner there is an apartment house several stories high, I must know the number of your floor and your apartment in order to find you. This is the third perpendicular. But New Yorkers are often on the go. I can't find you unless I also know the *time* when you're at home. So that's a fourth dimension.

"Time does not flow, any more than space flows," wrote Professor Andrei Oumoff, a Russian philosopher. "It is we who are flowing, wanderers in a four-dimensional universe. Time is just the same measurement of space as length, breadth and thickness."

He seems to be saying that time is interchangeable with the three other dimensions we know. Here's what I think he means. After I go to your apartment and find you—on the sixteenth floor, say—we wonder just how high that floor is above the street (the length of the third perpendicular, in other words). The manager can't tell us. But he knows that the elevator travels at a uniform speed of ten feet per second. If we look at a stopwatch, and time the trip down from your floor to the street, we see that 16 seconds elapse. So we know the distance is one hundred and sixty feet. The watch has translated time into space, just as earlier cultures used to measure distances by the number of days' march needed to cover them.

We measure space or time in terms of space-time. We can't measure them in terms of a fourth dimension. If our whole world and universe should miraculously shrink to one-tenth its size, or become a hundred times as large, we probably wouldn't know it because all our yardsticks would change accordingly. If everything should move twice as fast (including all our bodily processes), we'd think our speeded-up watches were keeping the same time as before.

We often see time stretched or squeezed in our three-dimensional world. A microscope may show us a microbe living a complete lifetime in a few seconds. We see a computer give us almost instant answers to intricate mathematical problems by turning switches a million times in one second. Some songbirds produce sounds faster than any human ear can follow; wren songs, tape-recorded and played back at slow speed, have proven that the wren sings 130 notes in seven seconds. The fact that we don't hear them all is merely proof that our sensory equipment isn't geared to that time scale.

Contrariwise, a few seconds can seem very long when you're in great pain. The same may be true during a happy dream or a nightmare. Drug takers say that ten minutes become several hours in their trance.

So we see that various mechanisms and organisms have time scales of their own—and that we ourselves experience a different kind of time in different physical and emotional states. The response of the vehicle establishes the time scale, just as the size of the body establishes the space scale. Time must be different for the ant and the thousand-year redwood tree, just as space is different. Maybe both are different in a multidimensional world.

I can believe that time is bendable as well as compressible, if it's part of a higher space. Here's what I mean, if analogies can make it clear.

Imagine yourself in a railroad train. You approach, reach, and pass through whatever stations are intersected by its track. You get a view of the landscape that every other traveler shares. After you leave a station, you can't go back to it. Nor can you arrive at places farther along the line before the train itself does. I think time is like a train, in our three-dimensional space.

Now suppose you change from the train to an automobile. In effect you have the freedom of a new dimension. You can return to stations the train has passed, or reach stations before the train does.

In normal time, you must travel along one line at a given rate. In hyperdimensional time, you can strike out in any direction and regulate your speed at will. This is hard to imagine, of course, because our brains aren't hyperdimensional.

Consider another example. You're on a street corner watching a parade. You see it as a sequence of bands, floats, and marchers coming suddenly into view, and disappearing as suddenly. This represents our ordinary waking consciousness of what happens to us in our three-dimensional world.

Now suppose you walk along the street in the same direction the parade is moving. Its "events" reach you much more slowly, or even "happen to you" in reverse order.

Next you walk in the opposite direction. The "events" go past you twice as fast.

And now if you take a shortcut, you can intercept the parade again at its midpoint or at its start. In effect you curve through time. To put this another way, time—the parade—curves and you angle across its route.

In another dimension you can see the whole parade at once—from a balloon. Past, present, and future merge into one. We know of a child prodigy who actually experienced something like this: Wolfgang Mozart. He was a European celebrity at the age of six. As an adult he said of his manner of composing: "I see the whole of it in my mind at a single glance. I do not hear it in my imagination as succession—the way it comes later—but all at once, as it were. All the inventing goes on in me as in a beautiful dream."

Today no one knows how Filippo Brunelleschi was able to construct his great dome of Florence Cathedral without centering, nor how Michelangelo could limn his mighty figures on the wet plaster of the Sistine vault with such extraordinary swiftness and skill. But we have their testimony that they invoked and received supernatural help. Presumably this was what enabled them to transcend ordinary limitations of space and time.

Maybe, without knowing it, we all possess sensory and intellectual equipment that would help us see and do the seemingly impossible. I think we're still evolving.

Here's one reason I think so. In chapter 14 I mentioned that the prehistoric cave painters used no green or blue. This was because they were partly color-blind, as most animals are today.

Even two thousand years ago our ancestors had very little color perception. Xenophanes described rainbows as having just three colors: purple, red, and yellow. Even Aristotle spoke of the tricolored rainbow. Democritus knew only black, white, red, and yellow. Homer apparently thought the sea was the same color as wine. Similarly, primitive Indo-European speech has no words at all for colors.

Today we see more colors than our forebears could, but we still see only a small segment of the spectrum. Likewise we're deaf to high ultrasonic sounds heard by dogs, and very deep notes. But our perceptions may keep improving as we evolve.

Maybe our mental powers will too. Maybe we'll develop whatever it is that already enables a few child prodigies and other gifted people to perform phenomenal feats without much training. There are tales of eastern wise men who are capable of teleportation. Can this be another inborn capability that our friends in outer space have evolved?

Even if shortcuts through space-time, through a

multidimensional universe, are mostly a matter of technology rather than talents, I suspect that they are possible. Let me offer one more analogy.

In New York are two apartment buildings, back to back. The entrance to one is on Fifth Avenue, the entrance to the other on Sixth. Mr. White and his wife live on the seventh floor of one of those buildings. A wall of their living room is the back wall of the building.

Their friends the Blacks live on the seventh floor of the other building, and a wall of *their* living room is the back wall of *their* building. So these two couples live within two feet of each other, since the back building walls actually touch. But of course they don't see or hear each other.

When the Blacks want to visit the Whites, they walk from their living room to the front door. Then they walk down a long hall to the elevator. They ride seven floors down. Then, in the street, they must walk around to the next block—and the city blocks are long. In bad weather they sometimes actually take a cab. They walk into the other building, they go through the lobby, ride up seven floors, walk down a hall, ring a bell, and finally enter their friends' living room—only two feet from their own.

The way the Blacks travel is like our civilization's space travel—the actual physical crossing of enormous three-dimensional spaces. But if they could only step through those two feet of wall without harming themselves or the wall—well, maybe that's how the old ones come here from their mysterious planet. Maybe they don't cross space, they avoid it.

I suspect that's the real explanation of whatever happened at Lake Titicaca and Tiahuanaco. I suspect that's how the people came here who built those long-dead cities in the Andes and Egypt, who made those enormous markings in the Peruvian desert, who mapped our world before map making was possible, who mastered whatever mysterious forces have been at work in the Bermuda Triangle or in an Egyptian pyramid. I suspect it's how so many great religious leaders just rose up and disappeared, as the legends have it; they went into other dimensions.

Man is incomplete, as the sages have said. Maybe he's the three-dimensional shadow of his full five-dimensional self.

In which case the best is yet to come. Someday we'll be more alive, more awake than any creatures we've ever known. Meanwhile it's up to us to keep flexible, keeping wondering, keep guessing, right up to the top of our highest hopes and a little beyond—and if we'll keep on making still one more daring guess, then our guess will come true beyond anything on Earth, beyond anything that we could ever have guessed.

That's what we have to do. And I guess we will.

# Bibliography

Abbott, Edwin A., *Flatland*. New York: Dover.

Alexander, Hartley B., *Latin-American Mythology*. The Mythology of All Races, vol. 11. New York: Cooper Square Publishers, 1964.

Anton, Ferdinand, *Art of Ancient Peru*. New York: Putnam's, 1972.

Asimov, Isaac, *New Intelligent Man's Guide to Science*. University of Toronto Press, 1965.

Beck, William S., "The Riddle of Life" in *Adventures of the Mind*. New York: Knopf, 1960.

Bellamy, Hans Schindler, *The Calendar of Tiahuanco*. London: Faber and Faber, 1956.

Bragdon, Claude, *Explorations into the Fourth Dimension: Four Dimensional Vistas*. New York: CSA, 1972.

Breasted, James H., *Ancient Times: A History of the Early World*. Boston: Ginn and Company, 1916.

Casson, Lionel, *Ancient Egypt*. New York: Time-Life Books, 1965.

Casson, Lionel, "The Search for Imhotep." *Horizon*, summer 1969.

Claiborne, Robert, and Goudsmit, Samuel A., *Time*. New York: Time-Life Books, 1966.

Clark, Kenneth, *Civilisation*. New York: Harper and Row, 1970.

Clarke, Arthur C., *The Promise of Space*. New York: Harper and Row, 1968.

Clarke, Arthur C., *Report on Planet Three: And Other Speculations*. New York: Harper and Row, 1972.

Cottrell, Leonard, *Lost Worlds*. New York: Doubleday, 1962.

Darwin, Charles, *Autobiography and Selected Letters*. Reprint of 1892 edition. New York: Dover.

Disselhoff, Hans-Dietrich, and Linne, Sigvald. *Art of Ancient America*. New York: Crown, 1961.

Dunne, John William, *The Serial Universe*. London: Faber and Faber, 1933.

Durant, Will, *Our Oriental Heritage*. New York: Simon and Schuster, 1935.

Eiseley, Loren, *The Immense Journey*. New York: Random House, 1957.

Eiseley, Loren, *The Night Country*. New York: Scribner's, 1971.

Eiseley, Loren, *The Unexpected Universe*. New York: Harcourt, Brace, Jovanovich, 1972.

Hale, John R., *Age of Exploration*. New York: Time-Life Books, 1966.

Hawkes, Jacquetta, and Bothmer, Bernard V., *Pharaohs of Egypt*. New York: Harper and Row, 1965.

Herrmann, Paul, *Conquest of Man*. New York: Harper and Row, 1954.

Howard, Cecil, and Parry, J. H. *Pizarro and the Conquest of Peru*. New York: Harper and Row, 1968.

Hoyle, Fred, "When Time Began" in *Adventures of the Mind*. New York: Knopf, 1960.

Hyams, Edward, and Ordish, George, *The Last of the Incas*. New York: Simon and Schuster, 1963.

Kaempffert, Waldemar, "Science and the Imagination" in *The Armchair Science Reader*. New York: Simon and Schuster, 1959.

Keller, Werner, *The Bible as History*. Translated by William Neil. New York: Morrow, 1956.

Koestler, Arthur, *The Ghost in the Machine*. New York: Macmillan, 1968.

Lindaman, Edward B., *Space: A New Direction for Mankind*. New York: Harper and Row, 1969.

Leopold, A. Starker, *The Desert*. New York: Time-Life Books, 1962.

Marden, Luis, "Titicaca: Abode of the Sun." *National Geographic*, February 1971.

McMullen, Roy, "The Lascaux Puzzle." *Horizon*, spring 1969.

Mumford, Lewis, *Technics and Civilization*. New York: Harcourt, Brace, 1934.

Mumford, Lewis, "How War Began," in *Adventures of the Mind*. New York: Knopf, 1960.

Newman, James R., "Einstein's Great Idea" in *Adventures of the Mind*. New York: Knopf, 1960.

Ouspensky, P. D., *A New Model of the Universe*. New York: Knopf, 1934.

Palmer, R. R., *Atlas of World History*. New York: Rand McNally, 1957.

Pauwels, Louis, and Bergier, Jacques, *The Morning of the Magicians*. New York: Stein and Day, 1964.

Prescott, William H., *History of the Conquest of Peru*. New York: Random House, 1963.

Priestly, John Boynton, *Man and Time*. New York: Dell, 1968.

Schurz, William, *This New World: The Civilization of Latin America*. New York: Dutton, 1954.

Smith, Ray Winfield, "Computer Helps Scholars Recreate Egyptian Temple." *National Geographic*, February 1971.

Sullivan, Walter, *Quest for a Continent*. New York: McGraw-Hill, 1957.

Thornton, Ian W., *Darwin's Islands*. Garden City, N. Y.: Natural History Press, 1971.

Toynbee, Arnold, "Cities in History" in *Cities of Destiny*. New York: McGraw-Hill, 1968.

Toynbee, Arnold, *A Study of History*. Oxford: Oxford University Press, 1947.

Velikovsky, Immanuel, *Earth in Upheaval*. New York: Doubleday, 1955.

Velikovsky, Immanuel, *Worlds in Collision*. New York: Doubleday, 1950.

Von Frisch, Karl, *Man and the Living World*. Translated by Elsa B. Lowenstein. New York: Harcourt, Brace and World, 1963.

*Anthropology Today*. Edited by CRM Books editorial staff. Del Mar, Calif.: CRM Books, 1971.

"Project Cyclops." NASA Ames Research Center, 1971 summer faculty project report in engineering systems design.

# Index

Abdullah al-Ma'mun, Caliph, 108-9
Abraham, 142
Adam, 141
Aegean Sea, 76
Aesculapius, 91
Africa, East, 159
Akbar, 124
Akhenaten, *see* Ikhnaton
Akhetaton (Horizon City) (Egypt), 127-30, 131
Alexander the Great, 102, 150-52, 170
Alpha Centauri A and B, 14
Altamira (Spain), 167-68, 170
Altiplano (High Plain) (Peru), 24, 25, 45, 52
Aluminum, 20
Alvarez, Louis, 99-100, 114
Amazon jungle, 35, 69
Amen, 122-23, 125, 126
Amen-Re, 123
Amenhotep II, Pharaoh, 122
Amenhotep IV, Pharaoh, *see* Ikhnaton
American Indians, 145
Andaman Islanders, 158
Anderson, Roger, 137-38
Andes Mountains, Indians of, 26, 29
  *See also* Incas
Andronikos of Kyrrhos, 21
Andros Island, 71, 74-77
Antarctica, 146, 147
Anthes, Rudolf, 105-6
Antipodes, 146
Apollo space flights, 45, 103, 138
Aqua-lung, 74
Arabs, 108-9
Arctic Circle, 146

Arctic Ocean, 146
Aries constellation, 15
Aristotle, 147, 184
Armenia, 21
Arrhenius, Svante, 3
Art
  Cro-Magnon, 166-71
  Egyptian, 128-29
Asclepieion, 94
Astronomy
  Egyptian, 106-7
  Great Pyramid and, 110-14
  Nazca lines and, 65
Atacama-Peruvian Desert, 58-69
  line patterns on (Nazca lines), 59-69, 76, 185
Atahualpa, 47
*Atalanta* (British ship), 83
Atlantis, 46, 73, 133
Aton, 123-25, 127, 129-31
Australia, 146, 158
Australian aborigines, 158
Avenger bombers, 79
Ayar Cachi, 142
Aymara language, 26
Azores Islands, 146
Aztecs, 48-50, 117, 119

Babylon (Babylonia), 21, 117, 148, 150
Bacchylides, 142
Baffin Bay (Greenland), 145
Bahama Banks, 72, 74-75
Bahama Islands, 69-72, 74-77
  *See also specific islands*
Bahama plateau, 85
Bellamy, Hans, 41
Bennett, Wendell C., 30, 55
Berblinger, 152

building of, 44-46, 52, 55-56
  granite blocks in, 39-40, 45, 77
  as unfinished, 44
  carved faces on walls of, 40-41, 54-56, 67
  Incas and, 40, 42-44, 46, 48-49
Tikal IV (Mayan temple), 117
Time, space and, 176-78, 181-85
  *See also* Fourth dimension
Timex, 6
Titicaca, Lake (Peru), 24-27, 34-36, 39, 48, 185
Titus Canyon, 68-69
Toltec pyramids, 117-18
Toltecs, 49, 119
Tongue of the Ocean (Bahama Islands), 71-72, 74
Tools
  Cro-Magnon, 166-68
  stone, 159-60, 163, 166
Torto, Juan, 152
Toth Pyramid, 101
Tower of the Winds (Athens), 21
Toxodon, 43
Toynbee, Arnold, 130
Tqurt, 122-23
Tutankhamen, pharaoh, 130-31
Tutankhaton, 130-31

Ultima Thule, 145

Unidentified flying objects, 18-20
U.S. Naval Observatory, 113
U.S. Navy, Flight 19 case and, 78-80
Ur ruins (Mesopotamia), 75
Ural Mountains, 168

Van Allen belts, 3, 135
Viracocha, 47-50, 52-56, 76
Virgil, 142

Wad'i, 123
Wallace, Alfred Russel, 157-59, 169
Warshofsky, Fred, 8
Weeping God, 41-43, 56, 59
White, Larry, 7
Whitman, Walt, 180
World War I, 84
Writing, Thoth as inventor of, 97-98

Xenophanes, 184

Yahweh, 141

Zana Valley (Chile), 69
Ziggurats, 117
*Zinjanthropus (Zinj)* ("East African man"), 159-62
Zoser I, pharaoh, 91, 92, 107
Zwicky, Fritz, 12

# A SELECTED LIST OF BOOKS ABOUT
# UFO's AND OTHER STRANGE PHENOMENA